Confessions of a Fundamentalist

Aaron Dunlop

Published by
Tentmaker Publications
121 Hartshill Road
Stoke-on-Trent
Staffs. ST4 7LU

www.tentmakerpublications.com

ISBN: 978-1-911005-07-0

CONTENTS

Dedication

To the memory of the elders of Lissara Presbyterian Church
(N. Ireland), and their families, who separated for the sake of
the gospel in March 1951.

Hugh James Adams
James Morrison
William Miscampbell
Cecil Harvey
George K. Gibson

To Mrs. Hannah Moffitt, and to the memory of her husband John,
who, as a young couple, stood on the side of the gospel.

To my parents, who, as second generation fundamentalists,
taught me to love our Lord and His church.

Foreword

The first time I exchanged words with Aaron Dunlop was to disagree with something he had written. He offered a kind and charitable response that opened both a larger conversation and a friendship. While he and I come from different cultures and have different histories, we share many of the same concerns.

The following small book began as a series of essays about fundamentalism on Aaron's blog. These essays were my first introduction to Aaron. They are where he and I began our conversation and our friendship.

Friendship does not entail the elimination of disagreement. Because our exposure to fundamentalism has differed, Aaron and I see things rather differently. As I've read the following chapters, I've regularly found myself saying, "Yes, but… ," or even, "I don't think so."

I've spoken to Aaron about some of these differences, and he has always listened carefully to my concerns. Usually, he has offered a reply that helped me to understand why he said what he said. Along the way, this exchange has helped me to sharpen and clarify some of my own ideas.

Aaron didn't set out to write a book. Friends from outside of the United States encouraged him to expand his original articles and to put them into print. He has been hesitant, and at one point even offered to bury the project if I advised him to. That I refuse to do.

Why? Among other reasons, because Aaron is doing fundamentalism a service by publishing this book. We will be stronger with it than without it. Specifically, this volume will help us in four ways.

First, in this book, Aaron reminds us of some of our highest ideals. While much of what he says is critical, he writes as a committed fundamentalist who wants to see all of us—himself included—live up to our best lights. He repeatedly brings us back to what ought to be our highest aspirations.

Second, the book expresses a widely-held perspective on fundamentalism. Even if that perspective is mistaken at some points—and I think it is—it's shared by many of Aaron's generation. It shapes their vision of and commitment to fundamentalism. To attempt to suppress the expression of this perspective is both foolish and futile. To ignore or dismiss it is simply to wish away most of Aaron's generation—a generation that fundamentalism needs.

What the perspective of this book requires is thoughtful response, the kind of response that can be offered only after respectful and careful listening. So I encourage readers to listen to Aaron, not so that they can disagree or refute him, but so that they can grasp his genuine concerns and understand why they are so important to him. His concerns are the concerns of a generation, and understanding him will help us understand his peers.

Third, this book will help older fundamentalist to know what they need to clarify. Its author has grown up within fundamentalism. He has been reared in fundamentalist churches and trained in fundamentalist schools. He pastors a fundamentalist congregation. If we think that his understanding of fundamentalist history, fundamentalist thinking or fundamentalist current events is skewed, we have no one to blame but ourselves. If we think he is wrong, then it is our responsibility to offer, or even re-offer, publicly-accessible explanations that are better than the ones he has been given.

Fourth, and perhaps most importantly, a book like Aaron's will help us to remember how accountable we are. As Christians—as *fundamentalists*—what we are doing is not gamesmanship, posturing or partisan politics. It is deadly serious. A million years from now we will look back on our mortal lives, and we will see how our conduct in this present world influenced eternal destinies, including our own. As we read this book, we may sometimes wonder whether we aren't being held up to an unfair standard of judgement. Let us remember, however, that a day is swiftly approaching when we will face a Judge who knows our every deed and motive. I seriously doubt that his standard of judgement will be less strict than the one represented here.

Fundamentalism has attracted its share of destructive critics. I do not believe that Aaron Dunlop is among them. Whatever wounds Aaron's book inflicts will be the wounds of a friend. We should hear him out, carefully and thoroughly. When we reply, we should remember that we are conversing with someone who actually has our best interests at heart. Such a conversation is necessary, not only for Aaron and his generation, but for the future health of fundamentalism as a whole.

Kevin T. Bauder
Central Baptist Theological Seminary of Minneapolis
March 2016

INTRODUCTION

Fundamentalism is extremely complex. There are many sides to the movement, many conflicting identities within it, and it has manifested itself in many different forms since the prophetic conferences of the late 1800s. One writer has condensed fundamentalism into four distinct and successive forms: irenic (1893–1919), militant (1919–1940), divisive (1941–1960), and separatist fundamentalism (1960–present).[1] Through all of these periods there have been those known as "moderates" who, while holding to the fundamentals of the faith, followed a different path than that which the movement took. Even within the movement there are those who were more moderate in their defence of the faith. Their counterparts became known as the "fighting fundamentalists."

Most self-identifying fundamentalists today would describe themselves as "militant separatists." These two biblical doctrines—militancy and separation—have become the ideology of the movement, without which fundamentalism would not exist.

The branch of fundamentalism that I know best, and in which I grew up, is identified more with the so-called "fighting fundamentalists." I was born into a Free Presbyterian home—a pastor's son—just twenty years after the formation of that denomination and six years after the

---

1 John Fea, "Understanding the Changing Façade of Twentieth-Century American Protestant Fundamentalism: Toward a Historical Definition," *Trinity Journal* 15:2, Fall 1994: 181–199.

Paisley-Jones connection was strengthened by Ian Paisley's imprisonment. The relationship between Paisley and Bob Jones affected conservative Christianity in Northern Ireland more than any other outside influence.[2] I attended a Free Presbyterian, private Christian school and later graduated from two Free Presbyterian institutions: the Whitefield College of the Bible (Northern Ireland) and Geneva Reformed Seminary (Greenville, South Carolina, U.S.A.). I am a Free Presbyterian and am deeply grateful for my heritage in the gospel.

However, as the fundamentalist writer Earnest Pickering has said, "Honest fundamentalists must admit that some of their number have been guilty of excesses and unscriptural behaviour. Some have walked in the flesh and not the Spirit. Some have insisted that everyone with whom they fellowship must cross every t and dot every i in the same way that they do."[3] Pickering is not the only fundamentalist to make this admission, as you will read in the following pages.

By all accounts, fundamentalism as a movement has made many and significant errors, and as a consequence has suffered serious decline over the past forty years. As I look back over my history in the Free Presbyterian Church and in the fundamentalist movement, on both sides of the Atlantic, I have to agree with Pickering and acknowledge these "excesses and unscriptural behaviour." I have to recognise also that, in the absence of proper correctives and honest self-

---

2 Although Ian Paisley had links with Carl McIntire and the International Council of Christian Churches (ICCC) from the early 1950s, it was the links forged with Bob Jones University and the personal friendship with Bob Jones Jr. that had the most influence on Dr. Paisley, and consequently in Northern Ireland. It was this link, furthermore, that facilitated the rise of Free Presbyterianism in the United States. Ministers within the Free Presbyterian Church differ in their opinion on this Paisley-Jones relationship and its influence on the denomination.

3 Ernest Pickering, *The Tragedy of Compromise* (Greenville: Bob Jones University Press, 1994), 8.

examination, many injured believers have defected from their fundamentalist roots. Many of my own generation who grew up in the 70s and 80s have joined the ongoing defection. Friends and colleagues now attend or minister in churches that would not self-identify as fundamentalist and have joined the ranks of what is more broadly considered conservative evangelicalism—for which they have been bitterly criticised.

Furthermore, a new generation is coming of age and they are finding that fundamentalism is just as unattractive as those of my generation found it to be. The defection continues. Sadly, many within fundamentalism have chosen to ignore these facts and to deny the trajectory of decline. Others, blinded by their own self-assured standards and methodologies, welcome these departures believing them to be purifying. Others are genuinely concerned but are unable to identify the problem or understand it's complexities.

It is my contention that in "the struggle for a pure Church,"[4] fundamentalism as a movement has put heavy burdens on people that are too heavy to bear—and for too long, stifled freedom of thought and expression, smothered liberty of conscience for the sake of denominational identity, and encouraged passive cooperation over solid biblical investigation. These ills have only deepened, as the years progress. It is time for serious reflection.

The fundamentalist, typically, does not ask diagnostic questions. Sadly, the problem is always with those who leave. Some of us, however, ask why? Bob Jones Jr. once said, "True fundamentalism demands that a man settle certain things with the Lord and with himself and keep those things always before him."[5] Unfortunately, many fundamentalists have taken this to the point where they believe

---

[4] The subtitle of Ernest Pickering's book on biblical separation.
[5] Bob Jones, *Cornbread and Caviar* (Greenville: Bob Jones University Press, 1985), 167.

it is wrong to question anything! In the minds of many, freedom of thought and expression is equated with rebellion, and the rebellious (those who question or leave) are shunned with the same ire as apostates. Practices, values, and certain peripheral matters have taken on the same status as the verities of the gospel and these also became "settled" matters, with the same prerequisite—nothing can be revisited.

I believe that we have a duty to reflect on who we are in relation to the body of Christ and to examine our path for the future generations. In the pages that follow, therefore, I examine some of the key values that have developed within parts of the fundamentalist movement. I do not question the fundamentalist *idea*, or the theological verities that the fundamentalist defends. I take issue with certain methodologies and excesses that have evolved within parts of the movement.

I have good reason to take issue with these, and I would hope that every honest, right thinking fundamentalist would do so also when he understands that they impinge on the message of the gospel—on the liberty and enjoyment of the gospel. I don't write to condemn, but to correct. If my fundamentalist heritage has taught me anything it has taught me to stand boldly for the faith, not just to preach the gospel, but to protect it, and to raise my voice against anything that would corrupt "the simplicity that is in Christ" (see 2 Corinthians 11:3). Fundamentalism taught me to do this without fearing the face of men. This, by God's grace, is why I write.

The book is divided into nine chapters and an appendix. Chapter one deals with the history of the movement and its evident purpose and success in preserving the truth. Chapter two is an appreciation of the "conviction and courage" that was evident among fundamentalists. In chapters three to seven I wrestle with some of the problems of the movement, including, shallow evangelism and a tendency to legalistic holiness (three); the unrelenting and harsh militancy that developed into infighting and contentions and factions within the movement (four); the indiscriminate separatism (five); and the failure (or inability) to deal with these issues (six).

In chapter seven, I address the "silent moderate majority" who have sat back and tolerated (perhaps promoted) the excesses. Chapter eight is an analysis of the current situation developing between fundamentalism and conservative evangelicalism—the new conservative evangelical identify. In the last chapter, chapter nine, I present five suggestions for a way forward.

In the appendix I have tried to bring some balance in our understanding of the powerful personalities of fundamentalism. Three men, Ian Paisley (Northern Ireland), Carl McIntire (America) and T. T. Shields (Canada), represent the three countries where the fundamentalist movement existed. They were polarising individuals, either hated or loved. How can we understand these very complex men of God?

I do realize that there have been changes in many parts of fundamentalism in more recent days—I want to acknowledge this. I am aware also that friends and colleagues disagree with much of what I've written. Much of what I have written however, is auto-biographical, as the title suggests. It is an appraisal of fundamentalism from my own experience and the experience of others, as I show from the writings of other fundamentalists.

The content of this book first appeared on my own thinkGOSPEL.com blog, with no intention at that time of printed format. A number of people, however, have encouraged me to give this material a more permanent presentation in book form, which you now hold in your hand. A testimony, I believe, to the widespread desire for a fresh look at fundamentalism.

I want to thank a number of people for making this project possible. To numerous friends who encouraged the publication of this book and who helped to make it possible. To Allister Bonar for sourcing the publisher, and to Phil Roberts of Tentmaker for taking on the task of publishing. To Alister and to the Rev. Paul Thomson (Antrim Free Presbyterian Church) for their help in research in Northern Ireland and to David Johnstone for his assistance in the final production. To my Brother in law, Trevor Cunningham for his encouragement and my nephew Matthew Cunningham, a sophomore at Bob Jones University, for being on hand to check references in the BJU library. Also to Patrick Robbins in the Fundamentalist Files of Bob Jones University for his patience and assistance on my visit there.

I would also like to thank Janice Van Eck for her services as a copy editor. To Stephen Hogg and Pepper Collective for the cover design and typesetting. To Dr. Michael Barrett for reading the manuscript. To Dr. Kevin Bauder for his advice and friendship and for his willingness to talk through many of the issues and to write a foreword. To my dad, whose advice was always appreciated and mostly followed. Most of all I would like to thank my wife Grace for her support, patience and insight.

This book comes to you with thankfulness to God for the many fundamentalists who stood valiantly and preserved the faith for succeeding generations. Soli Deo gloria.

Aaron Dunlop

Victoria, BC.

March 2016

THE DEVELOPMENT OF A MOVEMENT

Very often when my children ask me for something they know they aren't likely to get, I will try to lighten the moment by asking them, "Do you want the short answer or the long answer?" The short answer, of course, is "No." The long answer explains why.

For many within the fundamentalist movement the question "Are you a fundamentalist?" needs the long answer. The reason for this is that fundamentalism is a nuanced web of historical, theological, and political complexities. You could throw into that mix a few prominent personalities.

The last thirty years have seen significant change in fundamentalist circles. Dr. David Beale, historian at Bob Jones University, identified this change as the "neo-fundamentalist defection into broad evangelicalism" which he says began about 1970. This defection has increased exponentially in the last ten years.

The last of the "fighting fundamentalist" leaders has gone on to glory and the movement is struggling to remain intact. Many more senior fundamentalists are struggling to move into a post-Christian context and the younger generation has no interest in going back to rehash old wars (the battle-lines have shifted). Many younger fundamentalists are thinking through the issues, some significant figures in the movement are writing about the current difficulties, some are trying to reform the movement, and large numbers are leaving. In 2015, three key fundamentalist schools were forced to close their doors. Fundamentalism is in decline, if it has not already expired. Those colleges that have survived have had to make substantial changes—perhaps too little too late.

The answer to the question "Are you a fundamentalist?" still poses problems for many who remain within the movement. Their responses balance gingerly on the difference between what fundamentalism was in its essential and historical purpose and what fundamentalism became as a major politico-religious movement. Let's start with a bit of history.

To understand fundamentalism, you need to know that it was a response to theological liberalism. It was a protest movement. Liberalism was a theological revolution that began in Germany in the early 1800s, spread through Europe, and made its way into the seminaries and universities of America. By 1900, as Eugene Osterhaven pointed out, "the transition had virtually been completed and the Liberal era in American theology had arrived."[6]

Liberalism was an anti-supernatural movement focused on a social gospel. It denied the authority of Scripture and other core doctrines of the Christian faith. It adopted a higher-critical approach to the text of Scripture, which worked on the premise that the Scriptures were mere human productions. Liberalism was—and is—an apostate system, and those who opposed it became known as fundamentalists because they held to the truths of Scripture which were considered

6 M. Eugene Osterhaven, "American Theology in the Twentieth Century" in *Christian Faith and Modern Theology*, ed. Carl F. H. Henry (New York: Channel Press, 1964), 48.

fundamental to orthodox faith. The term "fundamentalist" was coined by Curtis Lee Law, editor of a conservative weekly paper. In the July 1, 1920 editorial of his *Watchman-Examiner*, Law used the term to refer to those who were prepared to "do battle royal for the fundamentals."[7]

Liberalism affected every denomination and each denomination dealt with it in different ways. Some were swallowed up in its perceived wisdom and so-called scientific advancement. Others quietly weathered the storm or separated. Many of these still exist today as conservative evangelical independent churches or smaller denominations. The Plymouth Brethren, for example, isolated themselves from the other denominations and were unaffected by the theological discussion despite the fact that their brand of dispensationalism was very influential on early fundamentalist thinking. Pentecostalism, also, which was an anti-liberal protest movement, never became part of the broader fundamentalist movement, although in the early stages it presented itself as a very effective answer to the anti-supernaturalism that the liberals were touting.

In North America, however, fundamentalism developed into a major ecclesiastical movement that spanned a number of different denominations. The beginning of fundamentalism in America goes back to the late 1800s with a "proto-fundamentalism" (*circa* 1878–1914), which was heavily influenced by dispensational theology responding to liberalism by organizing Bible and prophetic conferences.[8]

---

7 Stewart G. Cole, *The History of Fundamentalism* (1963; reprint, Eugene: Wipf & Stock, 2008), 67.

8 Ronald George Sawatsky, "Looking for that Blessed Hope: The Roots of Fundamentalism in Canada 1878-1914" (Ph.D. diss., University of Toronto, 1985).

The tipping point, however, came in the mid 1920s when, after years of frustration over the double-speak of liberals, fundamentalism was forced to adopt a decidedly militant approach. The year to remember is 1927, when the first denominational splits took place. New churches were formed and a number of fundamentalist educational institutions were established across America and Canada. Fundamentalism had changed from a peaceful movement within mainline churches to a theological war machine that took no prisoners.

The only other country in the world where a fundamentalist movement developed was in Northern Ireland. Again, 1927 was a key year. Modernism had been making its voice heard for some time. For twenty years, Rev. James Hunter had made numerous protests against the Presbyterian Church in Ireland (PCI) and its close links with the United Presbyterian Church of Scotland.[9]

The first influences of American fundamentalism in Ulster came through the ministry of W. P. Nicholson. Nicholson had gone to America in 1918 and was employed at BIOLA (Bible Institute of Los Angeles). In the early 1920s he returned to Ulster and engaged in a series of evangelistic campaigns, which proved successful, indeed it has been claimed, "saved Ulster from civil war."[10] There is little doubt that Nicholson's fiery evangelistic preaching and attacks on liberalism influenced Ulster fundamentalist militancy beyond those gospel campaigns. Many were saved in those campaigns who later became involved in the PCI.

---

9 Finlay Holmes, *Our Presbyterian Heritage* (Belfast: The Publications Committee of the Presbyterian Church in Ireland, 1985), 153.
10 Holmes, *Our Presbyterian Heritage*, 152.

In 1925, Jim Grier, a young student from Donegal, Ireland, returned home after two years at Princeton Seminary, U.S.A. Grier had been saved in a Nicholson campaign in October 1922. As he settled into his final year of preparation for the ministry in the PCI, he found himself debating openly with the professors at Union College, Belfast. In December 1925, Jim Grier sought counsel from Rev. Hunter, and from this point the two men became close allies in the cause against liberalism in the PCI.

In 1927, Professor J. E. Davey of Union College was tried for heresy and acquitted. This was too much for Hunter and Grier so they left the PCI and formed the Irish Evangelical Church (it later became the Evangelical Presbyterian Church).[11] Grier had already been exposed to this controversy in America and his friendship with J. Gresham Machen—an important figure in the stand for truth in America—was influential in this early break from the PCI. Machen visited Belfast that same year. As in America, this early break from the PCI was moderated and non-sectarian.

Militant fundamentalism, as we know it, did not come to Northern Ireland until the early 1950s when Rev. Ian Paisley pursued a relationship with his American counterparts after the forming of the Free Presbyterian Church of Ulster. Paisley believed the mantle of Nicholson had fallen on him and he often recounted the incident from the first Sunday after his ordination at Ravenhill Evangelical Church. That Sunday morning, Nicholson approached the front of the church after the sermon and prayed that the young preacher would be given a tongue "as sharp as an old cow;" as sharp as a file

---

11 W. J. Grier, *The Origin and Witness of the Irish Evangelical Church*, (Belfast: Evangelical Bookshop, 1945).

that will "disturb hell and the devil." Paisley "believe[d] God answered his prayer."[12]

By the mid 1960s in Northern Ireland, fundamentalism had taken on the characteristics of a movement, albeit on a more limited scale (mostly among Free Presbyterians) and closely linked with the political struggle of that country (politics also played a role in America and to a lesser degree in Canada). The impetus for fundamentalism developing as a movement in Northern Ireland came with the imprisonment of Paisley and two of his associates for protesting at the General Assembly of the Irish Presbyterian Church.

Although the Free Presbyterian Church had begun in 1951, there was relatively little growth in the new denomination prior to 1966; only twelve churches had been established in fifteen years. During and after the 1966 imprisonment, rallies were organized across the country and interest in Paisley's movement gained momentum. Those churches established during or immediately after the three-month imprisonment became known as "the prison churches." In less than two years the number of congregations doubled and Paisley's new Martyrs' Memorial Church, seating 2,500, was under construction. "Paisleyites," as they became known, were finding their feet and making their voice heard all over the country.

The 1966 imprisonment raised the Paisley name to celebrity status not only in Northern Ireland but also in North America. Paisley had met Bob Jones back in 1962 at the International Council of Christian Churches (ICCC) conference in Amsterdam. When Bob Jones Jr. heard that Paisley had been imprisoned in Belfast he proposed to the Board of Trustees to "grant him the honorary degree Doctor of

---

12 Ian R. K. Paisley, *Sermons By W. P. Nicholson: Tornado of the Pulpit* (Belfast: Martyrs Memorial Publications, 1982), 10.

Divinity" to "encourage him."[13] Within days of Paisley's release, Bob Jones Jr. arrived in Ulster to confer the degree and to preach an evangelistic campaign. The imprisonment story was picked up by at least three fundamentalist periodicals in North America: in Canada, *The Gospel Witness* of T. T. Shields' fame, and in America, John R. Rice's *The Sword of the Lord* and Carl McIntire's *The Christian Beacon*. The following year, Paisley embarked on a tour of the U.S.A. and Canada. Beginning in Pennsylvania at the end of March, he was met at the Philadelphia International Airport by "several hundred hymn-singing supporters."[14] After meetings in the Bible Presbyterian Church he moved on to the annual Bible Conference at Bob Jones University. His name appeared in many local newspapers and was aired on radio programs across the nation announcing his meetings. In the October 1967 edition of *The Gospel Witness*, a portrait of the middle-aged Paisley covered the front page announcing a series of meetings that took him from the Canadian Maritimes in the east to Vancouver in the west. Paisley was now accepted into the fundamentalist "Hall of Fame" with honours.

This brief survey of the movement ties fundamentalism across three countries: America, Canada, and Northern Ireland. As I stated before, there was no fundamentalist *movement* outside these three countries, though there were isolated fundamentalist churches and organizations. This is an important observation, as one Canadian historian poignantly remarked: "There was no fundamentalist movement in England, and there is no church in England to speak

---

13 Bob Jones III, cited in David McIlveen, *This is My Friend* (Belfast: Bannside Library, 2015), 100.
14 Richard Lawrence Jordan, *The Second Coming of Ian Paisley; Militant Fundamentalism and Ulster Politics,* (New York: Syracuse University Press, 2013), 187.

of."[15] Apart from a few small and struggling churches, England has no unified evangelical voice.

Early fundamentalism was effective. Whether you agree with other aspects of the movement or not, this much is clear, as Iain H. Murray wrote: "Fundamentalism…cannot be easily ignored."[16] Both Northern Ireland and North America enjoy the benefits of evangelical truth that can be traced directly to the fundamentalist movement. This gives some perspective to the movement and should generate not a little gratitude for the stand that the early fundamentalists took for the "faith once delivered."

There were, of course, fundamentalists in England. Spurgeon separated from the Baptist Union in 1887 in what was called the "Down-Grade Controversy." What is significant about the Down-Grade Controversy, however, is that it had no lasting effect. Despite the fact that Spurgeon was so well received in the Baptist Union when he first came to London in 1854, he had little influence in the Union when liberalism appeared, and was the last and lone voice for Calvinist theology in late Victorian England.[17] There was little influence also from the American fundamentalists who succeeded Charles Spurgeon at the Metropolitan Tabernacle: A. T. Pierson (1891–1893) and A. C. Dixon (1911–1919).

Spurgeon's Down-Grade Controversy was a great embarrassment both to the Baptist Union and, it seemed, to many conservative Baptists in England. "Conservative Evangelicals" were considered

---

15 I have to thank Dr. Michael Haykin for suggesting this line of thought. Dr. Haykin has been a great help and I am very thankful for his kindness and friendship.
16 Iain H. Murray, *John MacArthur: Servant of the Word and Flock* (Edinburgh: Banner of Truth Trust, 2011), 59.
17 Iain H. Murray, *The Forgotten Spurgeon* (Edinburgh: Banner of Truth Trust, 1966), 176.

"obscurantists." In 1932 Dr. T. R. Glover, the liberal president of the Baptist Union in Great Britain and Ireland, wrote, "Today if you want a real old obscurantist college, you will have to found one," and in a reply to that, in *The Times* newspaper, a Methodist writer confirmed, "Today, in all seven English theological colleges of the Methodist Church the point of view known in America as Fundamentalism is not represented at all."[18]

By 1934 at the centenary celebrations of Spurgeon's birth, even Spurgeon's friends in conservative Baptist circles were embarrassed with the controversy and indeed implied that Spurgeon was to blame for leaving the Baptist Union. [19]

There were other attempts in England to organize a militant anti-liberal movement, such as that by John W. Thomas and the Baptist Bible Union, and E. J. Poole-Connor's fellowship of Independent Churches (1922). None of these movements gained significant traction. One reason suggested is that the English fundamentalists— D. Martyn Lloyd-Jones, J. I. Packer, and John R. W. Stott, to name a few—were "moderate." There were others not so moderate and even some closely associated with the American movement, but despite this, no movement as such formed in England, and the Northern Ireland movement had no real influence on mainland Britain.

Rather than call for separation, as the fundamentalists did, Lloyd-Jones, in the 1950s and 60s, called for an evangelical unity based only on the gospel.[20] Interestingly, today Lloyd-Jones' influence in England

---

18 E. J. Poole-Connor, *Evangelicalism In England* (Worthing: Henry E. Walton, 1966), 251, note 91.

19 David G. Fountain, *Contending for the Faith: A Prophet Amidst the Sweeping Changes of English Evangelicalism* (London: Wakeman Trust, 1966), 112.

20 "The Basis of Christian Unity" in D. Martyn Lloyd-Jones, *Knowing The Times* (Edinburgh: Banner of Truth Trust, 1989), 118–163. See also, Iain H. Murray, *Dr.*

is limited, although he is regarded with tremendous respect in the wider Reformed church, and deservedly so.

In the early 1970s, Lloyd-Jones changed his view on church unity and separation. His biographer points out that his "scope was deliberately narrowed" and he no longer "looked for a broad influence." Evidently Lloyd-Jones realized, as the fundamentalists had been saying all along—"'the remnant' principle of Judges chapter 7"—the way forward was for the "minority to stand fast and, in so doing, prepare the way to brighter days."[21]

In the March 2006 edition of *Tabletalk*, R. C. Sproul, Jr., wrote an article called, "Our Fundamentalist Betters." In that article he recognized the debt that the evangelical church owes to the fundamentalists. Sproul says, "The fundamentalists of the last century were ... scorned. And for that they earned the praise of Jesus." The "contendings and tirades,"[22] to quote Lloyd-Jones, paid off and preserved the strong evangelical presence that we enjoy today.

Reformed and evangelical churches in Northern Ireland and in North America can thank the fundamentalists for standing up and screaming, "Foul!" when others kept silent, recoiled into their own comfortable constituency, or focused on the positives hoping the negatives would disappear. Although very much a voice in the wilderness (e.g., less than 1% of the Protestant population in Northern Ireland), it cannot be ignored that the "religious right" has

---

Martyn Lloyd Jones: The Fight of Faith (Edinburgh: Banner of Truth Trust, 1990) 427–450.

21 Iain Murray, *Dr. Martyn Lloyd Jones: The Fight of Faith,* (Edinburgh: Banner of Truth Trust, 1990), 673.

22 *Ibid,* 530.

been an active political and spiritual force in America, Canada, and in Northern Ireland.[23]

The fundamentalist movement had many and serious faults, which I hope to address in later chapters. There was much that the movement failed to achieve within its own ranks, but it must be recognized that the noise of battle made others sit up and listen and that it "prepared the way to brighter days." Conservative evangelicals are enjoying those "brighter days" today.

---

23 In a 1983 sermon, Dr. Paisley said, "The Free Presbyterian Church of Ulster has been the only Church to challenge the apostasy of Irish Presbyterianism" (*The Revivalist*, June 1983: 31). See also Ian Paisley, *For Such a Time As This* (Belfast: Ambassador-Emerald, 1999), 46. Speaking on the subject of Presbyterianism in Northern Ireland, Paisley said that after the Presbyterian Church in Ireland (the largest protestant denomination), there are three smaller Presbyterian groups: Non-Subscribing Presbyterian Church (Unitarian), Reformed Presbyterian Church (Covenanters), and the Evangelical Presbyterian Church. Dr. Paisley continued, *"The Free Presbyterian Church is not only the largest of these three smaller [Presbyterian] denominations but is larger than all three put together."*

CONVICTION, COURAGE AND
BIBLICAL AUTHORITY

At the end of December 2000, I arrived in Albertville, France, with just enough French to identify myself and be courteous— *bonjour, s'il vous plaît, et merci.* I had enrolled for a twelve-month language course in an evangelical missionary language school about an hour and twenty minutes south of Geneva in the foothills of the French Alps. Those attending the school represented a wide variety of evangelicals from around the world, mostly Americans, although there were some from South Africa, Australia, Ukraine, Brazil, and England.

Some of the classes toward the end of the course were designed to encourage and indeed force us struggling French-speakers to use our newly acquired language. In those classes we were forbidden to speak English, and the professor, a very wise man, chose subjects that were theologically charged, emotive subjects like abortion, euthanasia, and the role of women in the church.

The choice of subjects had its desired effect, at least on me and on my American friend Jim. We threw in our two-cents worth in our very broken French. We became known for our persistent and dogmatic dependence on the text of Scripture and were mocked by some for it.

In one particular debate, which will forever remain etched on my memory, a British lady was so irate at my insistence on Scripture that she broke into the forbidden English in a fit of rage having exhausted not only her patience but also her French vocabulary.

While I look back on that incident with a little humour, those were traumatic days for me. It was a time of real heart-searching. For the first time in my life I was receiving unsolicited exposure to broad evangelicalism—and it wasn't at all pleasant! I discovered there the reality of what John MacArthur said a few years ago concerning his own ministry: "Never did I believe that I would spend most of my life trying to rescue the gospel from evangelicals."[24]

Many evenings I went back to my room in confusion, wondering whether I was right in being so persistent and dogmatic in upholding biblical verities. I asked myself, *Did I frame my arguments correctly? Was I holding the truth in love? Is there another way to do this? Why can't I just sit and keep my mouth shut?* I always came back to the same conclusion, as I said in class regularly: "It doesn't matter what I say, but what does the Bible say? ...If the Bible is offensive, then take it up with the Author."

I have taken the time to relate that scene because I believe it is analogous to the broader fundamentalist struggle. It was intense and difficult at the time but, as I consider it now over fifteen years on, I realize that I was simply being a fundamentalist. Furthermore, although my friend Jim probably would not have identified himself with that movement, and fundamentalists would not have accepted

---

[24] This statement was made in a September 2004 interview with Kirk Cameron, http://www.gty.org/video/interviews/INT-KC-01. This statement was repeated in a "*Five Minutes in Church History*" interview with Stephen Nichols on January 26, 2016; http://5minutesinchurchhistory.com/deserted-island-top-5-john-macarthur; accessed January 27, 2016.

him as one of their own because of his associations, yet he also was being a fundamentalist—in the broader (and original) use of the term.

I will never forget what one of my fellow students said to me as I prepared to leave that language school at the end of 2001. After thanking me for taking my stand in the classes, he said (I paraphrase), "I could not do that. I'm too afraid, but I agree with you and I admire your courage."

If my experience in that French language school mirrors that of the fundamentalist, could my friend's confession of fearfulness mirror that of many other conservative evangelicals? Theologically, he agreed with the fundamentalist, he admired the fundamentalist's courage but was unwilling or afraid to stand up and be heard, or even align himself publically with me, "the fundamentalist." He had the convictions of a fundamentalist but lacked the courage needed to defend those convictions.

I learned there that while many evangelicals may mock the excesses of fundamentalism and distance themselves from the militancy—even a biblical militancy—they admire the courage and conviction of those who stand.

I learned that many evangelicals are like the timid boy cowering in the corner of the school playground—they are happy for someone else to do the fighting for them. If the other guys get a black eye, then it's all good. This is what R. C. Sproul Jr., meant, essentially, when he spoke of "Our Fundamentalist Betters."

I have learned also that while it has "become fashionable in evangelical circles to join in criticism of 'Fundamentalism,'" as Iain Murray said, there are those who have left and who look back to their fundamentalist heritage with respect and admiration. In 1951, Billy

Graham interviewed Dr. Bob Jones Jr. in his *Hour Of Decision* radio broadcast. As he introduced Jones he made this statement:

> Bob Jones University is a School which I went to fifteen years ago, and it was there that I first learned about evangelism. It was there that I first received my passion for the souls of men, and began to realize the desperate need of a world outside of Christ."[25]

Others, while they no longer associate with fundamentalism, are ready to come to its defense, to recognize the biblical authority from which the fundamentalist gets his conviction and courage.

Examples of commendation for fundamentalism by evangelicals and by those who would not self-identify as fundamentalists are not at all hard to find.

On November 20, 1997, Moisés Silva, a well-known biblical scholar, delivered the presidential address to the Evangelical Theological Society in Santa Clara, California. In that address, Silva took James Barr to task for his 1977 book *Fundamentalism,* which is an all-out attack on the inerrancy and authority of Scripture. Silva, himself a graduate of Bob Jones University (1966) and, ironically, whose admiration of Barr's linguistic abilities "knows no bounds," reprimanded Barr for the anger and contempt so evident in the book and for "comments border[ing] on slander."[26] At one point in the footnotes of the presentation, and under no obligation, Silva even came to the defense of Bob Jones University.

---

25 Cited in Ian R. K. Paisley, *Billy Graham and the Church of Rome* (Belfast: Martyrs Memorial Publications, 1970), 41.

26 Moisés Silva, "'Can Two Walk Together Unless They Be Agreed?' Evangelical Theology and Biblical Scholarship" in *Journal of the Evangelical Theological Society* 41.1 (March 1998): 3–16.

Robert L. Reymond, author of *A New Systematic Theology of the Christian Faith,* studied at Bob Jones University and began his teaching career there in the 1960s. In a footnote, in the first few pages of his systematic theology where he deals with divine revelation, Reymond quotes the now famous words of a theological liberal, Kirsopp Lake, in defense of fundamentalism's stand on the authority of Scripture:

> It is a mistake often made by educated persons who happen to have but little knowledge of historical theology to suppose that fundamentalism is a new and strange form of thought.... I am sorry for the fate of anyone who tries to argue with a fundamentalist on the basis of authority. [27]

John Piper has an interesting history in fundamentalism. His father once served on the Bob Jones board of trustees and Piper himself has often defended fundamentalism. About ten years ago the Fundamental Baptist Fellowship International (FBFI) made a resolution against John Piper for, among other things, not separating from the Baptist General Conference for its toleration of Open Theism. Piper had already published against the heresy but that was not enough for the FBFI.

Piper has taken a bold stand on many issues, not least against Open Theism. On his Desiring God website, Piper has made some very clear statements in defense of fundamentalism, especially with regard to fundamentalists' conviction, courage, and appeal to biblical authority:

> What I want to say about Fundamentalism is that its great gift to the church is precisely the backbone to resist

---

27 Robert L. Reymond, *A New Systematic Theology of the Christian Faith,* (Nashville, TN, Thomas nelson Publishers, 1998), 16, nt. 32.

compromise and to make standing for truth and principle a means of love rather than an alternative to it. I am helped by the call for biblical separation, because almost no evangelicals even think about the doctrine.

So I thank God for fundamentalism, and I think that some of the whining about its ill effects would have to also be directed against the black-and-white bluntness of Jesus. [28]

In an article titled "20 Reasons I Don't Take Potshots At Fundamentalists," Piper outlines what he believes to be the positive side of fundamentalism.[29] Some of the reasons are stamped with Piper quirkiness so I have picked out a few that relate to the subject at hand:

They believe that truth really matters.
They believe that the Bible is true, all of it.
They know that the Bible calls for some kind of separation from the world.
They have backbone and are not prone to compromise principle.
They put obedience to Jesus above the approval of man (even though they fall short, like others).
They believe in hell and are loving enough to warn people about it.
They resist trendiness.
They don't think too much is gained by sounding hip.
Everybody to my left thinks I am one.

---

28 John Piper, "Praise God for Fundamentalists";
http://www.desiringgod.org/articles/praise-god-for-fundamentalists; accessed January 11, 2016.
29 John Piper, "20 Reasons I Don't Take Potshots At Fundamentalists";
http://www.desiringgod.org/articles/20-reasons-i-dont-take-potshots-at-fundamentalists; accessed January 11, 2016.

This, on all accounts, is the legacy of fundamentalism. The fundamentalist knows who he is; he has no identity crisis. He stands inflexibly on the authority of Scripture and does not equivocate for fear of offending or to curry favour. It is this belief in the absolute authority of Scripture that gives the fundamentalist the courage of his convictions. I know this from experience.

Say what you will about the fundamentalist—and I have a few criticisms myself—the fundamentalist has stood his ground, maintained the orthodox faith and the centrality of the blood of the cross, and, as Iain Murray testifies, "Because they sought to be biblical, Fundamentalism retained gospel preaching and evangelistic urgency when it was disappearing from other churches."[30]

Fundamentalists have taken enough black eyes in the defense of the faith. It's time for those cowering in the corners of evangelicalism to show us how we should contend for the faith differently or better. It's time for the conservative evangelical to show himself brave in a "resurgent fundamentalism" and prove the power and authority of God's Word to which he claims allegiance. For those evangelicals who have taken a few knocks for the faith in recent years, fundamentalists give you credit—at least some of us do.

---

30 Murray, *John MacArthur*, 59.

THE DANGERS OF
THE FUNDAMENTALIST MENTALITY

A number of years ago I was speaking in a church on the subject of salvation. I made the point, as a side note, that salvation is not a one-time event, but that it is a process. In fact, the New Testament speaks of salvation using all of the tenses—past, present/continuous, and future, "I was saved," "I am saved" (justification), "I am being saved" (sanctification), and "I will be saved" (glorification).

A few days later as I sat in a restaurant with two fundamentalist preachers who had been present in the meeting and who were much older men than I, one of them cautioned me about speaking of salvation in this way. His fear was that it could confuse people. I admitted that I could have framed my thoughts differently, but I underlined the importance and benefit of seeing the full biblical perspective of salvation from the Scriptures. Thankfully, the other gentleman came to my defense.

In some church circles it is customary to preach specifically to Christians in the morning worship service and to preach a dedicated "gospel" (i.e., evangelistic) message in the evening service to the unconverted. This practice developed in cultures where the unsaved would attend the evening service rather than the morning, which is no longer the case. On two occasions now after Sunday evening services I have been questioned as to why I did not preach "the gospel"!

On one occasion, just prior to the service, the minister asked my subject matter. I gave him the title of my sermon and he said, "Do you not preach the gospel on a Sunday evening?" I replied, with a light-hearted smile, "I preach the gospel every time I preach" and, without further comment, we made our way to the pulpit.

On another occasion, after preaching on the subject of glorification from 1 John 3:1–3 and, incidentally, with an unsaved friend in the meeting whom I had invited, I was asked at the door by a young lady, "Do you not believe in preaching the gospel on a Sunday night?" My reply to her was, "What do you think you just heard?"

While these three incidents were in a congenial atmosphere, they betray a limited, if not an unbiblical use, of the words "salvation" and "gospel." These incidents bring to the surface the idea that the gospel is a message for unbelievers and that believers need some sort of post-gospel message, a different message. In short, one might say, "I've heard the gospel; I'm saved. Now just tell me how to live as a Christian."

On the face of it, this statement might seem quite biblical. However, two problems arise out of it in the context of the fundamentalist movement: a shallow evangelism and a tendency to legalistic holiness.

Ironically, the early fundamentalist movement had a keen interest in the conversion of sinners and a high regard for personal holiness. However, perversions of these two virtues have become fundamentalism's greatest danger. In many areas of the movement, both evangelism and personal holiness degenerated into empty forms without a sound and exegetical foundation. Holiness became a mere form, a list of "do's and don'ts," and evangelism became an invitation to "accept Jesus" without a clear understanding of the depth of original and personal sin or the glory and fullness of what sinners are invited to in the gospel.

Before I address these two areas of evangelism and holiness, let me say something about the reason for this shift from principles to empty form: the lack of exegetical foundation.

Fundamentalists have always been very principled people. The problem is that the movement became so principle-driven that a fundamentalist mentality formed outside of a biblical framework. According to E. J. Carnell, an early New Evangelical, the "capital mistake" that converted fundamentalism from a "movement to a mentality" was that, "unlike the Continental Reformers and the English Dissenters, the Fundamentalists failed to connect their convictions with the classical creeds of the church."[31] Carnell again:

> The mentality of fundamentalism is dominated by ideological thinking. Ideological thinking is rigid, intolerant and doctrinaire; it sees principles everywhere, and all principles come in clear tones of black and white. It wages holy wars without acknowledging the elements of pride and personal interest that prompt the call to battle; it creates new evils while trying to correct old ones.[32]

The principles, however noble, were often not based soundly on biblical exegesis but on isolated proof texts. There are many examples

---

31 J. E. Carnell, *The Case For Orthodox Theology* (Philadelphia: The Westminster Press, 1959), 113–114.
32 Carnell, *The Case For Orthodox Theology*, 114.

of this. Let me give you just one: the notion that Christians shouldn't do anything that might look to anyone else like sin. The verse that was used to defend this principle is "abstain from all appearance of evil" (1 Thessalonians 5:22). This is a misinterpretation of the verse. Interestingly, in a 1962 evangelical magazine, on the same page as an article by one of Western Canada's most prominent fundamentalist leaders, a young Elisabeth Elliot wrote an article, "What is really meant by 'appearance of evil?'" to try to correct the interpretation.

After providing some examples from Scripture of occasions when men and women did things that "looked like sin" but were not, Elliot presented a number of different translations of 1 Thessalonians 5:22 and concluded that Paul is saying, "Test everything, discern, keep that which is good, but avoid every form of evil." Elliot reminded readers,

> Decisions must be made in the integrity of the heart before God—with an unselfish attention to our brother's good and the glory of God.... Let us not be Pharisees in our certainty of what God could or could not permit.[33]

The problem of proof-texting biblical principles arose because fundamentalists were typically afraid of academics and learning. After all, it was scholarship that had brought in liberalism and destroyed the church. For this reason, as a general rule, fundamentalists avoided academics. I had a pastor say to me once, "I don't need to read history; all I need is my Bible." I was shocked at this statement initially, but as time went on I realized that it illustrates very well the sort of mentality that has become such a part of fundamentalism. Unfortunately, this sort of statement forgets that the Bible *is* history and redemption is revealed through history.

---

33 Elisabeth Elliot, "What is really meant by 'appearance of evil?'" *Sunday-School Times*, Vol. 104, No. 13 (March 31, 1962): 237.

Kevin Bauder, one of the most prolific writers on fundamentalism today, writes,

> Part of the fault lies with fundamentalists themselves. For a generation or more, they have produced few sustained expositions of their ideas. Perhaps a certain amount of stereotyping is excusable, and maybe even unavoidable. No fundamentalist has produced a critical history of fundamentalism. Nor is any sustained, scholarly theological examination of core fundamentalist ideas available. [34]

As a result of this lack of biblical/theological investigation and self-examination, fundamentalism's most admirable characteristics—evangelism and personal holiness—degenerated into quibbles about makeup, hem lengths, and hairstyles, and evangelism turned into a mere invitation.

Let me address the area of evangelism and revivalism first. I recently spoke to a member of a fundamentalist church who is very discouraged by the shallow evangelistic preaching. He summed it up and, with a sense of hopelessness, said, "It's all invitation and no content." He may not have known it but this is classical revivalistic preaching.

Revivalism is what we might call free-style evangelism, closely associated with the techniques and "new measures" of Charles G. Finney (1792–1875) and more recently with the mass evangelism of Billy Graham. Revivalism erodes the theological foundation of the gospel, cheapens salvation, and focuses on the external results of

---

[34] Kevin T. Bauder, "Fundamentalism," in *Four Views on The Spectrum of Evangelicalism*, eds. Andrew David Naselli and Colin Hansen (Grand Rapids: Zondervan, 2011), 19.

evangelism. Numbers are crucial to the revivalist mentality and numerous methods are used to draw crowds. To that end, many churches have regular testimony slots in the evening meeting—celebrity testimonies especially are a big attraction—and of course a continuous flow of special music.

In the revivalistic mentality the effectiveness of the minister is determined by how many conversions he can chalk up to his ministry and these conversions are considered "God's seal" on his ministry. According to that rule, of course, Noah was a failure, and so were Ezekiel and Jeremiah, etc.

A few years ago a friend of mine was attending a fundamentalist church in Canada. On one occasion he inadvertently came within earshot of a Sunday school class one of his children was attending. The teacher was attempting to present the gospel. After establishing the fact that children are afraid of the darkness, the teacher described the scene of a potential car accident on the way home from church. In this hypothetical scene, both the parents died and the children were left without mom and dad. The application was forceful and manipulative. I paraphrase: "Don't you want to go to be with your parents and not be shut out into the darkness of hell forever?"

This is the type of shallow, fear-mongering evangelism that develops out of a lack-of-content gospel. It was the sort that many fundamentalists were quick to criticize in the Billy Graham crusades. It is the sort of gospel—the Jack Hyles' variety—that gets thousands up the aisle to accept Jesus only to discover that the Jesus they accepted was a hollow replica of the Christ of Scripture.

In his recent book *Stop Asking Jesus Into Your Heart*, J. D. Greear addresses the same subject. He chastizes the revivalistic, guilt-driven type of evangelistic preaching that demands of listeners an in-the-moment "decision for Jesus" and then leaves them confused. All of the clichés of this type of evangelistic preaching are dealt with: the "sinner's prayer," "asking Jesus into your heart," "getting saved." The main thesis that Greear presents is stated in the first chapter, "Salvation is not a prayer you pray in a one-time ceremony and then move on from; salvation is a posture of repentance and faith that you begin in a moment and maintain for the rest of your life."[35]

Greear states that the sinner's prayer is a biblical concept and that asking Jesus into your heart is not wrong in itself or unbiblical. His concern is that it is grossly misleading because it leaves so much out of what happens at conversion that is equally important: the sealing of the Spirit, the washing of the blood, one's name being written in the Lamb's book of life, etc. When Paul said that the "gospel is the power of God unto salvation" he did not simply mean that the gospel brings us to God, but, to use the title of Derek Thomas' recent book, it is the gospel that "brings us all the way home."[36]

The second area that lacked sound biblical footing in the fundamentalist ethos was personal holiness. The two fault lines are linked. In the absence of a full gospel message, where Christ is not only Saviour, but Sanctifier, through his Holy Spirit, something has to replace that agent of sanctification. Fundamentalists very often replaced spiritual growth in grace with a moral code of their own, which was culturally and sociologically mandated. Don't get me wrong. For the most part, the personal holiness of the fundamentalists was sincere and well-intended. Nonetheless, the

---

35 J. D. Greear, *Stop Asking Jesus Into Your Heart: How to Know for Sure You Are Saved* (Nashville: B & H Publishing, 2013), 5.
36 Derek Thomas, *How The Gospel Brings Us All The Way Home* (Lake Mary: Reformation Trust Publishing, 2011).

holiness of many fundamentalists was reduced to what we *do*, not what we *are*.

Here again, the fundamentalist mentality comes to the surface as a superficial (not based on Scripture but on culture and sociology), judgemental spirit that manipulates the unsuspecting to conform to a particular code and outward appearance. In some cases, modesty was not taught as a biblical principle but as a cultural more.

Worldliness very often became geographically defined. There are things that were counted "worldly" in certain parts of the world that were not considered to be so in other parts. In the 1970s and 80s worldliness looked different in Britain than it did in North America, and it still does today. Consider men's hairstyles or ladies' cosmetic makeup for example. In the 1970s men in Britain wore their hair longer than they do today, often covering their shirt collars. In North American churches this was shameful and in some colleges it was forbidden to wear the hair touching the ears or shirt collar. In the 1970s also, conservative Christian ladies in Britain shunned cosmetics as worldly while their North American counterparts painted it on in abundance, encouraged by one of their leaders, Bob Jones Sr., who famously said, "If the barn door needs painting, paint it."

To obey the command, "love not the world," the fundamentalists took the easy path and emphasized conservative living rather than biblical thinking. Scripture demands, however, that we try the spirits (1 John 4:1), search our hearts (Psalm 139:23), and inform our minds (1 Peter 1:13). The point is clear: worldliness is not always as overt and identifiable as one might think. Furthermore, the command to "love not the world" is not only obeyed by distancing oneself from certain activities and objects in the world or by entrenching oneself in a particular form of Christianity.

Worldliness is not so much what we *reject* of this world—the material things, the pleasures, or the fashions; it has more to do with how we *respond* to the influences of the world around us. It is not so much about right *living* as it is about right *thinking*; not so much about *things* as it is about *thoughts*. R. B. Kuiper wrote:

> There is a type of worldliness which is extremely prevalent in the church today and is doing untold damage, yet is hardly recognized as worldliness.... It is to count greatness as the world is wont to, to stress externals at the expense of spiritual values. [37]

37 R. B. Kuiper, *The Glorious Body of Christ*, (Edinburgh: Banner of Truth Trust, 1967), 15.

THE ACHILLES HEEL OF
FUNDAMENTALISM

Fundamentalism never wavered from its original purpose to defend the faith. This was its greatest virtue and the reason for its success in leaving us "brighter days." Despite the merits of fundamentalism, however, and its evident success, the movement developed quite a prominent Achilles heel.

As I said in the introduction, fundamentalism was an extremely complex movement. Historians differ on its crystallizing points. There are significant ecclesiastical considerations: its non-denominationalism was a contributing factor. There are also theological considerations: a strong dispensational pre-millennialism played a large part in its growth. Others see the core of fundamentalism forming around educational institutions (schools, colleges, and universities) or mission agencies, conferences, and the many publishing houses and fundamentalist periodicals that came into existence.

It is clear that fundamentalism was never a homogenous movement and it is equally clear that all of the factors mentioned had their part to play in its growth. But what caused it to grow into the divisive movement that was marked by infighting and schism? What was the impetus of the aggressive isolationism that developed in its ranks when ecclesiastical separation became the preferred method of dealing with secondary issues?

Why did some fundamentalists—more "moderate" in their temperament—distance themselves from the more radical or militant fundamentalists? I'm thinking now of men like J. Gresham Machen, Francis Schaeffer, J. Oliver Buswell, Robert Reymond, and more recently, John MacArthur Jr. There were also men like Martyn Lloyd-Jones in England and, in Northern Ireland, W. J. Grier of the Evangelical Presbyterian Church and Revs. Ivor Lewis and Donald Gilles of the PCI.

Ian Paisley had been preaching in the Evangelical Presbyterian Church before his ordination. He said of W. J. Grier, "He was a very close friend of mine when I was a student, and an encourager of me in those early days."[38] Grier preached Paisley's ordination sermon in 1946. However, just a few years later, in the early 1950s, Grier actively distanced himself from Ian Paisley and eventually from Carl McIntire in America also.[39]

As militant fundamentalism began to gain traction the "mainline fundamentalists" (those who stayed in the mainline denominations) came under increasing pressure to leave their denominations. But many of those who remained believed that they had good theological reason for remaining in the liberal-dominated denominations, and they also had good historical precedent. The Presbyterian Church in Ireland, out of which there were two fundamentalist splits (1927 and 1951), is a good example of this. Those fundamentalists who stayed in

---

38 Ian R. K. Paisley, *The Revivalist* (November 1986): 6.
39 Richard Lawrence Jordan, *The Second Coming of Paisley: Militant Fundamentalism and Ulster Politics* (New York: Syracuse University Press, 2013), 122.

the denomination believed "God could turn it around" and they remained in as an "influence for the evangelical position."[40] This confidence in the sovereignty of God was based on the knowledge that God had reformed the PCI during the previous century when it was controlled by Arianism.[41]

There were other reasons why these more moderate men stayed within their denominations and distanced themselves from the fundamentalism. By far the most common reason for this distance was that many moderate men felt that their form of fundamentalism was too bombastic, clamorous, and abrasive, as Lloyd-Jones famously explained to T. T. Shields in Toronto. Some moderates also perceived the fundamentalist leaders to be power-hungry "ecclesiastical adventurers."[42]

There was also the fact that fundamentalism developed alongside political ideologies both in North America and in Northern Ireland. In North America, fundamentalism became closely allied with the politics of the anti-communist movement and the struggle against America's foreign policy regarding the Soviet Union and China. In Northern Ireland, militant "fighting fundamentalism" developed in connection with the political struggles and the threat of a united Ireland, which coincided with an antipathy towards Roman Catholicism. In Canada, William Aberhart from Alberta founded the Social Credit Party during the Great Depression of the 1930s, and, during World War II, T. T. Shields became more politically active against the Roman Catholic province of Quebec. Shields' political

40 Interview with Rev. R. J. Coulter, January 27, 2016.
41 Interview with Rev. Willard Kelly, August 10, 2015. Also interviews with retired PCI minister Rev. Noel Agnew, August 11, 2015, and Rev. Martin Smith, January 28, 2016.
42 Jordan, *The Second Coming of Paisley*, 122.

aspirations did not come to anything.[43] More moderate men, whose only interest was the church, did not involve themselves with the political activism of the fundamentalists.

These reasons and many more could be given to explain the distance between the "moderate" and "fighting" fundamentalists. But there is a more basic answer to these questions. There was one characteristic that undergirded the whole fundamentalist movement. That characteristic was both its strength and its weakness. It determined how the movement was born, how it developed, and also, how it has ended. It is the "war psychology"—the Achilles heel of fundamentalism.

One historian put it this way, "The distinguishing characteristic that made fundamentalism a unique subset of American evangelicalism in the 1920s was not doctrine but the *attitude toward the defense* of such doctrine."[44]

This "war psychology" was born out of a uniquely intense period of church history and developed in many respects as a matter of pragmatism. Prior to the First World War, there was an "irenic fundamentalism."[45] It was not separatism that made the distinction between *irenic* and *militant* fundamentalism. Many historians trace the militancy of fundamentalism in North America to the post-war years and identify in it a strong anti-German sentiment against the

---

43 In a letter to Dr. James B. Rowell, dated March 1945, Dr. Shields requested that Rowell stand in Victoria as a candidate for Parliament. Shields had hoped that if he could get men across the country, he could form a government. No reply has been found and Rowell never indicated his desire for political office.

44 Fea, "Understanding the Changing Façade of Twentieth-Century American Protestant Fundamentalism," 187. Emphasis added.

45 Fea, "Understanding the Changing Façade of Twentieth-Century American Protestant Fundamentalism," 181–199.

German war machine and Friedrich Schleiermacher, the German theologian known as the "father of Liberal theology." George Marsden, who is not alone in this observation, asserts "the crusading spirit of the war, together with the urgency of cultural alarm that followed, contributed to the intensity of the fundamentalist reaction."[46]

In those early days, emotions were running high. There was an intense feeling of urgency and therefore a definite change of approach. Common sermon titles at this time were "War on Liberalism," "The Great Gulf Fixed," and "The Line in the Sand." In 1925 T. T. Shields, the most prominent Canadian fundamentalist, preached a message in New York entitled "The Necessity of Declaring War on Modernism."[47] The Baptist Bible Union published a booklet (circa 1924) with the title *A Call To Arms.*

This "war psychology" was indeed well placed against the liberalism of that day. Remember, this was after forty years of liberals "paltering with words in a double sense."[48] These words, written by a Chicago "free-thinker" in the early 1920s show that even secular observers could see that liberals expressed their "views about God, Christ, the Bible, and the Church, in language of masterly vagueness and ambiguity."[49] War on liberalism was indeed necessary.

As the movement gained momentum, however, it developed a mentality of war and a corresponding sense of paranoia. The war

---

[46] George M. Marsden, *Fundamentalism and American Culture* (Oxford: Oxford University Press, 2006), 159.

[47] T. T. Shields, "The Necessity of Declaring War on Modernism," *The Gospel Witness*, Vol. 4 (June 21, 1925): 1.

[48] "A Free Thinker on the Fundamentalists," *The King's Business*, Vol. 14, No. 8 (August 1923): 823.

[49] "A Free Thinker on the Fundamentalists," 823.

psychology, then, was a reaction of fear and not grounded in faith. It was focused on the enemy (or enemies) and not on Christ and it very often confused the goal of the church. Fundamentalists became more fearful of liberalism than they were confident in the power of the gospel. In this subculture of suspicion, many fundamentalists became reactionary and more and more obsessed with preserving their cause rather than with preserving the truths on which their cause was founded. Like scared and immature soldiers, their fingers were always on the trigger and they were ready to fire, at times, as Francis Schaeffer points out, "treat[ing] the liberals as less than human."[50]

The "line in the sand" and the "great gulf fixed" attitude was fine when it addressed the liberal theology. The issue was clear. But it left many on the outside who, with a little patience, could have been brought along. While defending the truth, many of the leaders of fundamentalism failed to convince the undecided, to strengthen the weaker brother, and as a result many were abandoned to the "mercy" of the liberals.

It became evident as the movement gained momentum that there was more than "the faith" involved in the fundamentalist fight. There was personalities and power struggles, there was political and social interests (anti-Roman Catholic and anti-Communist activity), American and "Victorian" values, and very evident in Canada during and after World War II was the fight for British Protestant imperialism. In many ways these conditions informed and shaped the fundamentalist's fight for "the faith." It was the confusion of two kingdoms.

---

50 Francis Schaeffer, *The Church Before a Watching World*, in *The Complete Works of Francis Schaeffer*, 5 vols. (Carlisle: Paternoster Press, 1982), 4:156.

This became the hallmark of fundamentalism. Contempt and rhetoric often became the mood and method of dealing with opposition. At times, the "war psychology" was so intense that the fundamentalists had no scruples drawing the sword on their own Christian brothers. There was the "if you're not with us you're against us" attitude, which often led to a shunning of those who left the movement or even of those who simply took a more moderate approach. By the 1940s fundamentalism was no longer a coalition of churches that defended the faith against liberalism, but a series of fundamentalist factions.

The clearly defined black and white of the liberal controversy had too easily carried over into the evangelical fundamentalist church. Matters of indifference were held with dogmatism and many became shibboleths and points of division and separation. Francis Schaeffer said there was a tendency to "become absolutists even in the lesser points of doctrine" and a failure to understand the difference between "believing in absolutes and having an absolutist attitude about everything."[51] Another historian said concerning T. T. Shields in Toronto that "every issue, whether a matter basic to his faith or a problem of administration, was a 'test case.' He viewed life as a series of 'superlatives.'"[52] In short, there was a profound inability to deal with differences of opinion.

The habits learned in the heat of the controversy were never tempered or refined. Schaeffer continues, "When major differences developed among themselves [the fundamentalists], they continued to treat each other badly."[53] The history of fundamentalism therefore is littered

---

[51] Schaeffer, *The Church Before a Watching World*, 4:159.
[52] Donald A. Wicks, "T. T. Shields and the Canadian Protestant League, 1941–1950" (M.A. thesis, University of Guelph, 1971), 11.
[53] Schaeffer, *The Church Before a Watching World*, 4:157.

with division among the leaders (Jack Hyles, Bob Jones Sr., John R. Rice, T. T. Shields, Ian Paisley, and Carl Macintyre to name a few).

Furthermore, when this continued war against the liberals (who were happily disengaged from it all) and the power-hungry infighting among the leadership was going on, the attention was distracted from the people who mattered: those in the pews who had followed their leaders and separated for the sake of the truth. These are the grassroots of the church, the would-be "church of tomorrow," and their leaders and pastors were so engaged in a continued "war on liberalism" that they could not or did not establish a substantial or effective teaching ministry.

It goes without saying that holiness in this atmosphere was not based on biblical exegesis nor displayed by love to the brethren as taught in the second great commandment. Holiness took on more of a pharisaical appearance that majored on particular practices but lacked principled and exegetical instruction. Worldliness was very often defined by the length of one's hair, amount of makeup, style of dress, and, in some quarters, a superstitious adherence to the King James Version of the Bible became the measure of one's spiritual experience.

Defense of the objective faith and a few selective external observances became the hallmark of Christianity. In this atmosphere—a breeding-ground for spiritual pride—externals were often more important than personal growth in grace. There was an impatience to let people grow slowly and individually. While holding tenaciously to the truth, these hyper-fundamentalists forgot to hold the truth in love, and for many on the outside, this hardline, dismissive, and abrasive attitude became the face of Christianity.[54]

---

54 Rosaria Butterfield, *The Secret Thoughts of an Unlikely Convert: An English Professor's Journey into Christian Faith* (Pittsburgh: Crown & Covenant Publications, 2012), 4-5.

For the past number of years I have been working on a biography of one of the earliest fundamentalist leaders in Canada, Dr. J. B. Rowell. Rowell was involved in the very first official church split in North America in the fundamentalist/liberal controversy. It happened in Vancouver in June 1927. The next month Rowell was preparing to plant a church for the new denomination in Victoria. The interesting thing about Rowell, who died in 1973, was that, although a separatist, he never adopted the "war psychology" that many of his counterparts did.

In 1930 Rowell wrote an article for his local church magazine, *The Advent Evangel*, entitled "Fundamental but Failing Fundamentally."[55] In that article Rowell chastized those who held to the fundamentals but did not live the fundamentals in holiness of life and in love for the brethren. He began the article like this:

> We are inclined to pride ourselves in our loyalty to the truth, our belief in the fundamentals of the faith, but there is another side to this question of loyalty to the truth. We must remember our Lord who said, "I am the Truth."[56]

Rowell continued by saying that a fundamental of Christianity is "love." He writes, "Under the old covenant and under the new we have the statements: 'love covereth' (Proverbs. 10:12; 1 Peter 4:8)." According to Rowell, if we don't live fundamentally correct, no matter how fundamental we are, this lack of holiness and brotherly

---

Butterfield states, "The closest I ever got to a Christian during these times were students who refused to read material in university classrooms on the grounds that 'knowing Jesus' meant never needing to know anything else; people who sent me hate mail; or people who carried signs at gay pride marches that read 'God Hates Fags.'"

55 *The Advent Evangel* (June 1930): 3.
56 *The Advent Evangel* (June 1930): 3.

love will "sap the life from your soul and undermine the foundations of your faith, and then drive you into the wilderness of this world barren and desolate."[57] For many associated with fundamentalism these words were prophetic!

The fundamentalists did not have an equal balance between orthodoxy (purity of doctrine), orthopraxy (correct practice), and what John Stackhouse calls orthopathy (right affections).[58] Fundamentalism became a very cold, and at times, oppressive, place to be. A hard, judgemental, and disapproving spirit developed and the movement became indifferent to felt needs of the individual and very often the culture around it.

This is where many are today. For them, the wheels have come off the fundamentalist bus. Many have been left injured and scarred by the experience. Others have jumped off the bus with the sense of relief that they have escaped the clutches of a cult. Many feel a sense of shame and embarrassment associated with these excesses; they are struggling to correct old prejudices, mend the damage caused by harshness, and overcome the stigma of the movement to find their place in the church of Christ outside the fundamentalist subculture.

---

57 *The Advent Evangel* (June 1930): 3.
58 John G. Stackhouse, "A Generic Evangelical Response," in *Four Views on The Spectrum of Evangelicalism,* eds. Naselli and Hansen, 57.

THE FLY IN THE
FUNDAMENTALIST OINTMENT

A few years ago, when Dr. Paisley made some very uncharacteristic political choices, the whole of Britain and Ireland, indeed the worldwide media, buzzed with the news. I also was surprised, and, like a good Ulsterman and expat, I had my opinions. Ironically, I was in Northern Ireland at the time doing research on fundamentalism and I preached for Dr. Paisley in his church in Belfast. Some wondered how I could disagree with Dr. Paisley and still preach for him.

To my mind the answer was very simple. Unlike many who publicly and vigorously disagreed with him, I found that my differences with Dr. Paisley did not impinge on my relationship with him and did not diminish my respect for him as a preacher of the gospel. Although I still had many questions, I could disagree with him without separating from him.

The question of what biblical ecclesiastical separation is has become pivotal in fundamentalism. Along with its "war psychology," fundamentalism's view of separation has become one of its most unfortunate characteristics. It has taken separation to outrageous lengths, failing to analyze it in the light of history or to base it on sound biblical exegesis, instead constructing its foundation on a number of misused Scripture "proof texts."

In the early days of the movement, in order to be a fundamentalist you had to first be theologically orthodox. Today there is another prerequisite: militant, aggressive, and indiscriminate separation. I believe in biblical separation, but separation is not a test of orthodoxy, it is not a fundamental of the faith, and it should never have become so dominant as to characterize the movement. Fundamentalists separated over separation.

Furthermore, with many fundamentalists, separation has become the first and only choice for dealing with the slightest differences. In the fundamentalist mentality, disagreement on any level and on any issue constitutes a good reason for ecclesiastical separation. They disregard the possibility that some areas of separation could, and should be, dealt with on a case-by-case basis.

In some cases, personality clashes and power-struggles even became the impetus for separation. This is why fundamentalism as a movement evolved from a coalition of churches holding mutually to the core doctrines of Scripture into a group of factions within a broader movement. This is the fly in the ointment.

The place to begin to understand the fundamentalist mentality on separation is the 1920s and 30s. The teaching of the church on separation prior to this time was very different. Read John Calvin's letters and see the spirit of catholicity; notice George Whitefield's acceptance of John Wesley; observe the Anglican J. C. Ryle during his bishopric in Liverpool. Read the life of Charles Spurgeon and see the inter-church relations practiced in London during his tenure at the Metropolitan Tabernacle. How was their practice of separation different from what we know today?

I have already noted one difference in a previous chapter: unlike their predecessors, the fundamentalists "failed to connect their convictions with the classical creeds of the church." There's another difference. The church splits of the late 1920s and early 30s were so novel, so ground-breaking, and so traumatic that many of that generation never recovered from the trauma. Christendom had not seen such a divisive period since the time of the Reformation. Whole ministries were shaped by the battles of the 1920s and by its atmosphere of antagonism. The antagonism of that period became the soul of fundamentalism in later years and shaped the way many fundamentalists viewed others in the broader Christian church.

Many were never able to move on to the next battle, or to adjust the level of aggression to what was appropriate according to the seriousness of an issue. Because every issue was a crisis moment in the church, many could not see the dangers that were up ahead for the next generation. For many young people (second and third generations) growing up in fundamentalism, church history consisted of learning about the battles of the "first generation fundamentalists," rehearsing the 1920s and 30s. Many fundamentalist young people grew up with annual celebrations of the fundamentalist/liberal controversies, and the stories of the skirmishes, stunts, and protests entertained the crowds of second generation fundamentalists who gathered to hear them.

This rehashing of the old battles left the fundamentalist church anemic and intellectually impotent for the present battles. Where are the fundamentalists in the battle against evolution, Open Theism or the charismatic movement? It is the conservative evangelicals who are leading the charge on current debates.

If these words, attributed by some to Martin Luther, are true, one has to wonder how "faithful" fundamentalism really is today:

If I profess, with the loudest voice and the clearest exposition, every portion of the truth of God except precisely that little point which the world and the devil are at that moment attacking, I am not confessing Christ, however boldly I may be professing Christianity. Where the battle rages the loyalty of the soldier is proved; and to be steady on all the battle-field besides is mere flight and disgrace to him if he flinches at that one point.

The doctrine of separation, which had been very much a black-and-white issue in the context of liberal theology, remained black and white in every issue. Every issue that arose in the church became a test case and a reason for separation.

Scriptures that are used by fundamentalists today to defend the doctrine of separation are often taken out of context and interpreted exclusively within the parameters of the modern fundamentalist struggle. Many fundamentalists who coldly and dogmatically "refused to defile themselves" (Daniel 1:8), ignored the gracious manner with which Daniel dealt with his situation.

For the fundamentalist to have fellowship with a group or individual (unless that person was already a fundamentalist, for, as we shall see, fundamentalists are very forgiving of their own), every detail of the life of the church or the individual had to be scrutinized: the books one read, the music one listened to, and the hymns that churches used. Everything was under the microscope and one became guilty even on the basis of a loose association with what was considered to be unacceptable. New terms were coined or borrowed to perpetuate this unbiblical doctrine of separation, terms such as "platform fellowship" and "associational compromise."

Furthermore, the doctrine of separation very often became extremely censorious and degenerated into a discussion about everyone else. The fundamentalists were not emphasizing what they believed to be right—their focus was on the presumption that everyone else was wrong. This hyper-separatist view passed judgement on everyone else's standing with the Lord, their orthodoxy, and their experience of God. Many were so busy trying to correct the ills of others and of the broader church that they neglected their own glaring inconsistencies (Matthew 7:5), their lack of fellowship and love for the brethren, and their own weak spiritual growth (1 Timothy 4:16).

Could it be that the brother who "walketh disorderly" (2 Thessalonians 3:6) is not necessarily the one who has a broad view of fellowship but the one whose doctrine of fellowship is too narrow, divisive, and schismatic? Could it be that the "disobedient brother" is not the one who is over-generous in his acceptance of others, but the one who lacks that gracious and magnanimous spirit? Could it be that those who have "caused division and offenses" are indeed the hyper-fundamentalists and that we should "avoid *them*" (Romans 16:17, emphasis added)? Could it be that the hyper-fundamentalists are the ones who have trespassed against their brothers and that it is these who need to be brought before the church (Matthew 18:15–17)?

These are the questions that fundamentalists need to ask and that our young people are already asking. Some think they have waited long enough for answers that haven't come and they are moving on. They have concluded that they can't get the fly out of the ointment, so the ointment has to go!

It has been often said that the doctrine of separatism has developed into isolationism. Over the years, fundamentalism in general has adopted a mentality of dogmatism, and narrowness that was not there in the beginning. The practice of separation has become increasingly stringent. It is true that Dr. Paisley often thundered with pulpit rhetoric and maintained a public persona as Ulster's "fire-brand preacher." He appeared in public more stringent than he was on a personal level. The fact is, Paisley was very open minded. Individuals from whom Paisley disassociated himself and hotly opposed publicly in the 1950s, remained his personal friends throughout his life. The same openness is also seen in his practice on separation.

Prior to 1951, Ian Paisley was a separatist fundamentalist minister fellowshipping with mainline fundamentalists (those fundamentalists who remained in the mainline churches). This was common in the early days of fundamentalism, on both sides of the Atlantic. The Ravenhill Evangelical Church had split away from the PCI a few hundred yards up the road. But Paisley, friendly with the Evangelical Presbyterian churches, was also preaching in the more liberal dominated PCI from which the Evangelicals had separated in 1927. It might surprise some to know that the Statement of Faith that the Free Presbyterians still adhere to was drawn up in the home of a Presbyterian Church in Ireland minister, Rev. Ivor Lewis.[59] One retired minister from the Presbyterian Church in Ireland, with whom Paisley was friendly states that "the earlier men [in the Free Presbyterian Church] were much more open in their fellowship and friendship."[60]

This 1979 sermon gives some indication of Paisley's breadth of fellowship:

> I say to all men who believe in the Infallibility of the Book, all men who believe in the Virgin Birth and the full Deity of the Lord Jesus Christ; all men who believe in

59 *The Revivalist* (May 1981): 8.
60 Interview with Rev. Willard Kelly, August 10, 2015.

the Vicarious Death and the Substitutionary Atonement of the Saviour and His Bodily Resurrection, and His Coming again in power and great glory; all men that believe that men depraved by sin need to be born again by the Holy Spirit if they would get to Heaven; all men that believe in what Thomas Chalmers said were the grand peculiarities of the gospel, the great fundamental principles of Christianity, all such men should unite today; and if I see another regiment in God's Army giving the Devil a hot time. I have time to cheer them on as I go into the battle. I am not going to turn my guns on them. [61]

In the earlier days of my own denomination, the Free Presbyterian Church, there was also more openness to fellowship with other churches and institutions. Browse through *The Revivalist* (the official denominational magazine) and note the many missionaries and missionary organizations that were receiving support from the Free Presbyterian Church. One individual who was part of the initial separation in 1951 states that the denomination is "not the same as it was." In fact, when asked what changes there have been over the years, she stated in good old-fashioned Ulster-Scots, "Oh, its n'more the Free Church than the man on the moon," [62] by which she means that the changes are so great that the Free Church (as it is affectionately known) today is nothing like the Free Church then, in

---

61 *The Revivalist* (May 1979): 8.

62 Interview with Mrs. Hannah Moffatt, January 7, 2015. Mrs. Moffatt is the daughter of Hugh James Adams. Hugh James Adams was one of the inaugural elders of the Free Presbyterian Church. When the Lissara Presbyterian Church (PCI) elders were suspended in alphabetic order, Hugh James Adams was the first. Mrs. Moffatt and her late husband (then a young couple dating) left the PCI and joined the split-away Free Presbyterian Church in 1951.

matters relating to attitude toward others and the centrality of the gospel, among other things.

In short, the church has become so consumed with the fundamentalist fight that it is in danger of losing sight of that for which it is fighting—the gospel. In some cases there is an inability to clearly articulate the fulness of the gospel, despite that fact that they militantly defend the faith.

Before I close this chapter with a parallel from history, it is worth noting that in the post-Christian culture we live in we are going to find natural centripetal forces bringing the Christian church together on the core values of the faith and especially on issues of Christian ethics.

This has already begun to happen. As I write this, just today in Belfast the Pentecostal pastor Rev. James McConnell appeared in court for a sermon he preached against the Muslim faith. Hundreds gathered at the court to support him and many from other denominations have posted their support on Facebook and other social media sites.

It was also seen in Belfast earlier this year in the legal action taken against Ashers Bakery by the Equality Commission of Northern Ireland. This affair brought the broader Christian community together in an unprecedented manner. Thousands from a variety of evangelical denominations congregated in one of Ulster's largest arenas, from Psalm-singing Reformed churches to experience-focused Pentecostal churches. The crowds were so large that many could not gain admittance and stood outside and sang hymns.

This is the type of Christian fellowship that happens only in an environment where people recognize a real danger to the church and not merely a perceived danger or the machinations of their own bigotry. Across the Western post-Christian world, we are going to see an escalation of these incidents. The church, the true church, will be forced to stand together and things that once separated us will be viewed in the future as insignificant, even stupid.

Let me finish with an illustration from history that in many respects points out a wrong-headed separatist mentality.[63] You will see from this illustration that today's fundamentalists do not have a monopoly on harshness and bigotry.

In 1746 the great Baptist theologian and preacher John Gill was ministering in London. At the same time the Anglican/Methodist evangelist George Whitefield was setting England alight with the gospel of saving grace. Christians today, who hold Whitefield in such high esteem, might be surprised to know that the great John Gill vigorously opposed any association with Whitefield's evangelism.

Some who opposed Whitefield referred to him as an "incarnate devil," an "enem[y] of God, Christ, religion" because he engaged in the uncommon practice of field-preaching and, it is supposed, was "too hasty in accounting the numbers of his converts." The irony is that many of the people sitting in the Baptist pews were converts of Whitefield. An unknown writer says,

> Sir, you and others cannot but be sensible, in the judgment of charity, that they have many seals of their despised ministry in your own churches.

In the letter addressed to Dr. John Gill recommending "unity among Christian ministers and people" the writer pleads with Dr. Gill to be consistent, to show the same grace to the Methodists with whom he

---

63 My thanks to Dr. Michael Haykin for suggesting this historical parallel.

disagrees as he shows to the Baptists with whom he disagrees. He pleads for a less bigoted and tribal mentality: "When will Judah no more vex Ephraim, nor Ephraim vex Judah?"

We learn a number of lessons from this parallel. First, tribal Christianity is no new thing! Second, just as many of the people in Gill's pews were converts of Whitefield, many of the people in fundamentalists' pews are getting their theological instruction from conservative evangelical ministries with whom their ministers would not fellowship. Third, many are critical of faults in others that they are willing to overlook among themselves. Gill was willing to treat Baptist faults with a leniency he was not willing to afford the Methodists. Fourth, when people look back to our day, will they wonder what caused good men in our society to keep such a distance and to speak so harshly of each other?

IS FUNDAMENTALISM
CHASING ITS OWN TAIL?

For the past forty years or more fundamentalism has struggled with its own existence. During that time fundamentalists have been discussing the nature and the future of a movement that was intended to defend the truth, but that has—some would argue—developed into a cold, impotent, and isolated subdivision of the evangelical church. This might sound harsh, but this is, in essence, what many fundamentalists have been saying of themselves for a long time.

Again, we must remember that fundamentalism is not a monolithic movement. George Marsden said "fundamentalism was a mosaic of divergent and sometimes contradictory traditions and tendencies that could never be totally integrated."[64] I am speaking of a certain category of individuals within the broader movement. Kevin Bauder, a professor at Central Baptist Theological Seminary in Minneapolis, calls them "the most visible representatives," the "noisiest" and, he thinks, "perhaps even a majority."[65]

---

[64] Marsden, *Fundamentalism and American Culture,* 43.
[65] Bauder, "Fundamentalism," 44.

In his 1986 book, *In Pursuit of Purity*, David Beale, then a professor of history at Bob Jones University, wrote of the "neo-fundamentalist defection into broad evangelicalism" which, he said, began about 1970. There were, of course, reasons for this "defection" and Beale identified one of them in another part of his book:

> Excesses and vagaries have frightened some Fundamentalists from the fountain of living waters. [66]

For many years now fundamentalist leaders have recognized that there were major problems in the movement. If you look through the last forty years of the movement you will discover that there have been some attempts at correcting these "excesses and vagaries," but they have been minimally successful. Ten years after Beale's book came out, David L. Burggraff, who was then the academic dean of Calvary Baptist Theological Seminary in Lansdale, Pennsylvania, predicted that the "centrifugal forces" driving people out of fundamentalism would only accelerate. [67] He was right, and the problems underlying those forces have not yet been corrected.

We should recognize that there have been attempts to correct. Back in 2012 Bauder wrote an open letter to Stephen Jones, then the president of Bob Jones University. In that letter Bauder commended Jones for what he described as "follow[ing] a trajectory of moderation and increasing responsibility." He pointed out that it takes courage to "acknowledge that some of the past commitments were overstated." [68]

---

66 David Beale, *In Pursuit of Purity: American Fundamentalism Since 1850* (Greenville: Bob Jones University Press, 1986), 358.

67 David L. Burggraff, "Fundamentalism at the End of the Twentieth Century," *Calvary Baptist Theological Journal* 11.1 (Spring 1995): 25.

68 Kevin T. Bauder, "An Open Letter to Dr. Stephen Jones," February 20, 2012, online at sharperiron.org; http://sharperiron.org/article/open-letter-to-dr-stephen-jones; accessed August 25, 2015.

Steve Petit, the new president of Bob Jones University, must also be commended for his courage in facing these issues and making tough decisions.

While some attempts at correction have been going on, in other quarters, an exorbitant amount of time and energy has been expended in defending the old fundamentalist bulwarks, rehashing old issues, reviewing the doctrine of separation, digging more trenches, and resolving to "keep on keeping on" rehashing, reviewing, and resolving.[69] What fundamentalism needs now is a vision for the future: a positive agenda for a struggling church in a post-Christian culture, grounding in biblical theology with all of its implications, and a return to the classical creeds of the church.

It seems to me that many in the fundamentalist movement have been running in circles looking for a way out, not sure that they really want to leave, or, if they *do* want to leave, being afraid to do so. Fundamentalism is like a dog chasing its own tail. Each year the same ground is covered, the same issues addressed, the same reminders made of who we are, and the same warnings given about who those are on the outside—with the same unwillingness to change, address concerns, or do anything productive.

It might surprise some to know that the World Congress of Fundamentalists was established for the distinct purpose (among other purposes, of course) of combating the attitudes and divisiveness that had resulted from the militancy fundamentalists proudly

---

[69] The theme of the Independent Baptist Fellowship of North America conference in 2014 was "Contending for the faith."
http://www.ibfna.org/v3/attachments/article/100/IBFNA%202014%20Brochure.pdf; accessed August 17, 2015. See also the lineup for the ACCC conference in October 2015.

practiced. The first congress met in Edinburgh, Scotland, June 15–22, 1976. The literature prepared for the congress asserted

> The militancy [of Fundamentalism] has tended to fractionalize and divide those who are united in their devotion to the "basics" in Christian doctrine. [70]

It is interesting that forty years ago fundamentalists were already talking about the same things: the underlying problems caused by fundamentalism's particular brand of militancy and the continued war psychology. It is also interesting, and not a little ironic, that at the 1990 World Congress in London, England, which I attended, the issue of this militancy directed at its own surfaced again, in meetings intended to bring peace. One of the speakers, among other faux pas, made a very derogatory and pointed comment about the doctrine of predestination. I recall the Calvinistic Ulster blood boiling as a result of that particular incident. It was reported that Bob Jones Jr. travelled across London that evening to the offender's hotel room to tell him to call his dogs off, as it were.

Did it not occur to the leaders of fundamentalism then that the problems could be corrected only by going to their root—the war psychology and the continued and pseudo-biblical articulation of militancy? Have the fundamentalists ever considered the root of the problem? They were always quick to tell others to be uncompromising and to "lay the axe to the root of the tree" (Matthew 3:10), but in matters which are dear to themselves and which they wear as a badge of honour, they have consistently refused to deal with it and have only patched over the damage.

---

70 *The Revivalist* (February 1976): 1.

At the World Congress in 1976, the fundamentalists promoted the same militancy that was splitting them apart. While one was saying, "This Congress is to emphasize the things on which we are united; we want to have fellowship," another was saying, "The need for such a Congress is everywhere apparent. The whole evangelistic arm of Protestant Christianity is in danger of splitting into either marshmallow soft neo-evangelicalism or stone-dead orthodoxy." The fundamentalists were going to correct the problem by

Expos[ing] and separat[ing] from all ecclesiastical denial of the Faith, compromise with error, and apostasy from the Truth; and earnestly contend[ing] for the Faith once delivered. [71]

This was part of the definition of a fundamentalist given at the 1976 Congress. It is a fine statement as it stands, but the fundamentalists' assumption was that to contend for the faith meant exposing everyone else's errors with placards and rallies, by shouting and extra-church activity.

I believe in "the Church militant" (1 Timothy 6:12), I believe that we must "hold fast" (2 Timothy 1:13), and "contend" (Jude 3) for the faith. The problem arises when our focus is so much on the enemy that it becomes a detriment to ourselves, our unity, and our enjoyment of the gospel. This is part of the root problem—our sights are always set on someone else. We have forgotten that theological error is not the only error to threaten the church and that while we are contending for the faith we must, as Jude reminds us, be "building up yourselves on your most holy faith, praying in the Holy Ghost, Keep yourselves in the love of God, looking for the mercy of our Lord Jesus Christ unto eternal life" (Jude 20–21). We must shift the focus

---

[71] *The Revivalist* (August 1976): 9.

off others and put it on ourselves. It will demand a rigorous spiritual encounter with God, a praying heart, and a loving life.

In 1993 James E. Singleton published a booklet called, "Fundamentalism: Past, Present and Future." As a self-described "student of history" Singleton had, according to the introduction in his book, "concerns about the movement he had given his life to further," and he could not ignore the faults.[72] Singleton's 25-page booklet is divided into three sections: "Where did we come from?," "How did we get to our present condition?" and, finally, "The Future of Fundamentalism." Singleton said the final part of his work was the most difficult to write because, he said, "Some feel in its present form that [fundamentalism] does not have a future."

Two years later in 1995, David L. Burggraff wrote a 31-page article for the *Calvary Baptist Theological Journal* entitled, "Fundamentalism at the End of the Twentieth Century." Two-thirds of his piece was devoted to outlining the history and development of fundamentalism, from the Irenic Movement (1860–1919) to Separatist Fundamentalism (1960–present). The last third of the article deals with "The Future of Fundamentalism and Evangelicalism."

According to Burggraff, fundamentalist leaders—at least some of them—were hearing the concerns that fundamentalism was "an individualistic, divisive and vitriolic movement."[73] But they were not listening. They admitted, "We have turned our weaponry on each other ... leaving fundamentalists wounded, bleeding, retreating and defecting." Burggraff confessed, "Young soldiers are reluctant to enter

---

[72] See PDF of this booklet online at
http://www.tricityministries.org/tcbc/resources/fundamentalism_booklet.pdf;
accessed August 1, 2015.
[73] Burggraff, "Fundamentalism at the End of the Twentieth Century," 25.

the battle where they fear they might be mistaken for the enemy and shot by one of their own."[74] What a shocking reality!

The brand of militancy and the war psychology that these men were wrestling with are the issues that young fundamentalists are still wrestling with today. However, there is one significant difference between then and now: the leaders around whom we rallied and to whom we looked are gone. Fundamentalism may have thrived best "when promoted by individuals who are charismatic."[75] But those leaders are all gone and the movement has begun to disintegrate.

Many of the colleges that North American fundamentalists call their *alma mater* are closed. Calvary Baptist Theological Seminary closed in May 2014. Clearwater Christian College closed its doors in June 2015. In March 2015, Tennessee Temple University announced that it would dissolve and merge with Piedmont International University in North Carolina. At the end of the 2014/2015 academic year, Northland International University closed its doors after a takeover by South Baptist Theological Seminary came to an abrupt and disappointing conclusion. These recent developments—and there have been others over the past decade—ought to cause any right-thinking fundamentalist to sit up and ask, "Why? Is there any relationship between these multiple closures and the nature of fundamentalism?" There must be some reason behind these defections, some underwhelming phenomenon beneath the surface—or perhaps *on* the surface—that repels.

There is a steady stream of men and women leaving fundamentalist churches, not because they no longer care about truth, but because they are unhappy with the excesses and imbalance and many see no

---

74 Burggraff, "Fundamentalism at the End of the Twentieth Century," 26.
75 Burggraff, "Fundamentalism at the End of the Twentieth Century," 25.

signs of correction. As these people leave, the question fundamentalists are asking is not "Why?" but "What's wrong with those who are leaving?" And there is an additional implied question: "How can the Lord call someone away from the fundamentalist movement?" The hyper-fundamentalist does not naturally think, *Is there something wrong with us?* Or, *Is there a problem with the movement?* These are questions the hyper-fundamentalist does not ask because the black-and-white mentality of the early controversy has been continued into every other area, and fundamentalists are uncomfortable with grey areas.

There are those in the movement who are happy to chase their tails and enjoy the dizziness of self-pursuit. There are those also who enjoy the militancy. They can't live without it, and cannot, or don't want, to live at peace with their fellow believers. There are others who nurse the martyr spirit and are happy to think themselves "the remnant."

Many recognize the problems, but will continue to plug the holes as they appear in the fundamentalist ship. Some see the hurt that has been caused but they have a deep-seated reservation against jettisoning the movement. What holds many back from identifying the "excesses and vagaries" as wrong-headed and indeed sinful, and from doing something about them, is, in part, the fear of man, which we all know brings a snare (Proverbs 29:25).

It is the fear of what certain colleagues will think, the fear of losing ministry opportunities if we are associated with this one or that one, the fear of being ostracized by our fundamentalist peers, the fear of disappointing our fundamentalist mentors, the fear of moving outside our comfort zone, the fear of leading others into broader pastures or uncharted waters, the fear of moving in circles where we will need to pray for more discernment, greater wisdom, and more grace.

The answer to fear of course is love: "For God hath not given us the spirit of fear; but of power, and of love, and of a sound mind" (2 Timothy 1:7). Broader fellowship and acceptance of others who differ, not in principle, but in certain practices or in the application of agreed principles, is the more difficult route, but it is the more biblical in that it enjoys the catholicity of the Church of Christ. It is also the more spiritual route in that it demands the engagement and application of "power, and of love, and of a sound mind" to make hard choices, to go into difficult areas, to be discerning and gracious.

FUNDAMENTALISM'S
SILENT MODERATE MAJORITY

In the first chapter I spoke of the legacy that the early fundamentalist movement has left to the evangelical church and suggested that conservative evangelicals enjoy better days today because of the fundamentalist struggle. I still believe that, and I will show the benefits and blessings of fundamentalism in North America and around the world in later chapters.

Before I get to that, I want to address one of the most complicated aspects of fundamentalism: the negative, oppressive atmosphere in the movement. I want to determine whether that negativity and oppressiveness is real or perceived. It is certainly real to some if the "neo-fundamentalist defection" is a reliable barometer.

I know many moderate men in the movement and from their actions and attitudes it would be impossible to perceive that there was anything wrong in the movement. And yet the general opinion of many on the outside of the movement is not positive, and if many people feel that way there must be some foundation for it. Why is that so? Why is fundamentalism viewed so negatively while many within the movement are actually moderate and mild-tempered?

Kevin Bauder is one of those moderates and perhaps the most prolific writer within fundamentalism today. In his contribution to *Four Views on The Spectrum of Evangelicalism*, Bauder gives a candid description of where he feels fundamentalism is today. Toward the end of his presentation, Bauder identifies eight incriminatory characteristics of what he calls "hyper-fundamentalism":

1. Loyalty to an organization, movement or leader. Anyone who criticizes the organization, or contradicts a leader is subject to censure or separation.

2. A militant stance on some extra-biblical or anti-biblical teaching; for example, those who teach that the King James Bible is the only acceptable English version.

3. Understanding separation in terms of guilt by association: "To associate with someone who holds any error constitutes an endorsement of that error."

4. "Hyper-fundamentalism is characterized by an inability to receive criticism...by an extreme defensiveness." To the hyper-fundamentalist any criticism constitutes an attack.

5. An anti-intellectualism; "some hyper-fundamentalists view education to be detrimental to spiritual growth."

6. Non-essentials are turned into tests of fundamentalism; "one's fundamentalist standing may be judged by such criteria as hair length, music preferences, and whether one allows women to wear trousers."

7. Hyper-fundamentalists often treat militant political involvement as a necessary obligation to the Christian faith. In the 1960s and 70s it was anti-communism but now many hold anti-abortion and anti-homosexual activism to be a necessary obligation to their faith.

8. Hyper-fundamentalists sometimes hold a double standard for personal ethics. Some things are permissible in their ecclesiastical warfare that would not be permissible in

ordinary life. They may employ name-calling, half-truths, and innuendo as legitimate weapons. [76]

After presenting a more moderate position as, what we might call "received fundamentalism," and after calling the hyper variety a "parasite on the fundamentalist movement," Bauder continues by saying this:

> Hyper-fundamentalism now constitutes a significant percentage of self-identified fundamentalists, perhaps even a majority. They have become the noisiest and often the most visible representatives of fundamentalism. They may be the only version of fundamentalism that many people ever see. [77]

I have a lot of respect for Kevin Bauder. His abilities are varied and impressive. He preached at my graduation from Geneva Reformed Seminary and, although I don't always read it, I subscribe to his *In the Nick of Time* blog with good intentions. However, it seems to me that if these eight characteristics identify the "majority" and the "noisiest" and the "most visible representatives," would it not be more correct to say that we are looking at *mainstream* and not *hyper* fundamentalism.

It should not surprise us that fundamentalism is viewed as the parasite on evangelicalism if hyper-fundamentalism—the parasite on fundamentalism—is the "majority" and the "noisiest" and the "most visible representative" of fundamentalism.

Take for example the American Council of Christian Churches (ACCC, a multi-denominational umbrella organization) and the

---

76 Bauder, "Fundamentalism," 43.
77 Bauder, "Fundamentalism," 44.

Independent Baptist Fellowship of North America (IBFNA). Both of these are major representative organizations of fundamentalism. After Bauder published in the Counterpoints Series, the ACCC issued a resolution that, while it didn't name him directly, cited his chapter and made it clear that it disapproved of his participation in the Zondervan project.[78] Dr. Kevin Hobi, an executive member of the ACCC, publicly wrote against Bauder in *The Review* (March 2013, Vol. 21, No. 3), an IBFNA publication.[79] In short, the problem for these institutions, was Bauder's "associational compromise" with other contributors. The ACCC did revise its resolution to something more moderate after Bauder answered his accusers in his *In the Nick of Time* blog. My point is, however, that they were critical of a fellow ACCC member and demonstrated such a negative spirit towards his participation in the project.

It is no surprise, then, that fundamentalists are viewed as contentious when organizations with such a wide public influence condemn one of their own—someone who is less extreme than they are—because they view him as a threat to the integrity of the movement.

There is another reason, however, a more subtle reason, why fundamentalism is viewed with such contempt. It is because the vocal minority, the radical, nitpicking, enth-degree separationists, speak for fundamentalism and fundamentalism lets them speak for it. Consider this in three steps.

First, the rightwing extremists (the "hyper-fundamentalists") are the most vocal and most visible representatives of the movement.

---

[78] http://www.accc4truth.org/images/Resolution_on_Neo-Fundamentalism_-_Fall_-_Final.pdf; accessed August 21, 2015. It should be noted that this resolution was revised after Dr. Bauder made some clarifications.

[79] http://www.ibfna.org/v3/attachments/article/95/The%20REVIEW%20March %202013.pdf; accessed August 21, 2015.

Second, the silent moderate majority holds to the truth and is happy to just do the work of God without raising concerns and without upsetting the fundamentalist apple cart. Their silence may seem commendable to some. It appears to be the more gracious option, the peace-keeping, conciliatory way forward. They may cringe and criticize their more radical brethren in private and even be open to change, but to do so publically would be deemed an attack on the movement—and so they remain quiet, conforming for the good of the system.

Third, this silent moderate majority offers the hyper-fundamentalist a certain protection in times of crisis. Fundamentalists tend to circle the wagons to support their own no matter how aberrant in theology or practice they are, while at the same time they are willing to attack others on the outside for a lot less. When push comes to shove, the silent moderate majority will invariably favour the extremist fundamentalist if it is a choice between him and a more moderate, or even a more faithful conservative evangelical. The reason for this is simply to protect fundamentalism, as Bauder points out in his first point.

For many looking on, this constitutes agreement with the extremists, perhaps a wall of protection or at least a buffer. Individuals are being hurt and the whole movement is identified by the belligerent vocal minority—and the majority in the middle acquiesces by its silence.

The safest course for the fundamentalist is to protect the movement and such protection often trumps truth and honesty. The same protection is not offered to the more progressive individual because he is viewed as a threat to the movement.

The grassroots people see these inconsistencies. The young men coming up in the movement also see them and they don't like it. It limits personal spiritual growth, it stifles the spirit of the Reformed principle *reformed and always reforming,* and it does not allow for acceptance of others. It creates an oppressive atmosphere. Dr. David L. Burggraff told us this way back in 1995: "Young soldiers are reluctant to enter the battle where they fear they might be mistaken for the enemy and shot by one of their own."[80]

The silent moderate majority has been silent for too long on the "excesses and vagaries,"[81] to quote Dr. Beale again, and have recoiled from speaking out against those who have been acting uncharitably against the body of Christ or those who have been guilty of behaviour not becoming of a Christian minister—because they are on the inside. This ongoing silence, which has in effect protected the extremist and his excesses, has caused irreparable damage. One wonders how far the "double standard for personal ethics"[82] that Bauder speaks of has gone at times and indeed how charitable Bauder has been in his choice of words.

Back in 1988 the fundamentalists were all over Dr. John MacArthur for his views on the blood and the nature of the atonement. Some of the wording that MacArthur used may have given a handle to his opponents, but he was for the most part teaching the same truths as the Reformers and Puritans—that the references to the blood are a metonym for the sacrificial death of Jesus—the blood sacrifice.[83] This

---

80 Burggraff, "Fundamentalism at the End of the Twentieth Century," 26.

81 Beale, *In Pursuit of Purity,* 358.

82 Bauder, "Fundamentalism," 43.

83 Thomas Adams, *The Works of Thomas Adams* (1861–1866, reprint; Eureka, California: Tanski Publications, 1998), 2:576–577. Adams argues that the word "blood" is used because, first, the blood is the life and that "death by the loss of blood is our redemption." Second, because "blood answers to the types of the legal sacrifices." In this view, Adams represents well the teaching of the reformers and Puritans.

was the teaching of an overwhelming majority of conservative commentators prior to Martin R. DeHann's curious teaching in his *Chemistry of the Blood* published in 1943.

I remember back to the later 1980s and early 1990s when books, tracts, and magazine articles were being circulated denouncing MacArthur for his views. The anti-MacArthur bandwagon had started rolling and the fundamentalists had jumped on with little or no historical research or exegetical insight. MacArthur was branded as an enemy of the gospel and, in some quarters of fundamentalism, an unsaved man! The damage caused by these unwarranted and slanderous attacks is still felt. Even today, young fundamentalists are asking, "Should we listen to John MacArthur?"

About the same time as John MacArthur was in the crosshairs of the fundamentalists, Dr. Jack Hyles, whose preaching was shallow entertainment at best and at worst a satire on the gospel, was still well received among fundamentalists. This was despite the serious questions regarding his theology and that he was ministering under a cloud of allegations of sexual immorality.

Cassette tapes of his sermons were being exchanged, his books were in circulation, and his sermons frequently used in fundamentalist pulpits. Even into the 1990s, I had friends who, on trips to America, would stop in to hear Hyles preach. What is worse, by 1998/99, when I came to do research for my college thesis, I wrote Hyles along with a number of other evangelical and Reformed leaders for primary source material. I was acting in ignorance of his sexual immorality and in naiveté regarding his ability to expound the gospel. My point is that he was accepted at the time as a fundamentalist even with all his theological and moral aberrations.

In the 2011 Preserving the Truth Conference, David Doran, Mark Minnick, and Kevin Bauder among others, engaged in an interesting discussion on aspects of fundamentalism. During that discussion the topic of the fundamentalist tendency to protect its own came up. Doran made this comment:

> We have tolerated aberrant doctrine and immoral behavior in the larger movement, in a way that, in times parallels what they [conservative evangelicals] have tolerated for greater good causes. [84]

When Minnick challenged him on this, he responded:

> Jack Hyles preached…in the pulpit in Greenville [SC]…well after he had preached the eternal humanity of Jesus Christ, well after people had suspicions about his moral behavior…. Now I don't think we're all culpable for that. But my point is to say…we hold *them* [conservative evangelicals] all culpable for the glitches on the other side.[85]

This reveals the inconsistency of the fundamentalists in protecting their own while ripping others into little pieces for "lesser" sins. Hyles, with all of his aberrant theology and his sexual misconduct, not to mention his empty gospel, was accepted because he was "one of us" while MacArthur was attacked because he was "one of them."

---

[84] http://www.fundamentallyreformed.com/2011/02/03/doran-minnick-bauder-discuss-fundamentalism-and-conservative-evangelicalism/; accessed August 18, 2015.
[85] http://www.fundamentallyreformed.com/2011/02/03/doran-minnick-bauder-discuss-fundamentalism-and-conservative-evangelicalism/; accessed August 18, 2015.

Robert L. Sumner, in his online fundamentalist paper *The Biblical Evangelist*, wrote concerning the labyrinth of sexual debauchery that Hyles constructed around himself while he was enabled by some to keep the lid on it:

> What can Fundamentalism and Fundamentalists do? For one thing, we can start standing up for what is right and opposing what is wrong, even—or especially—in our own movement. Perhaps we should forget the liberal Presbyterians and the compromising Convention Baptists for a season and concentrate on setting our own house in order. [86]

This is why fundamentalism has a bad name: they have been so concerned about others that they have ignored their own vineyard (see Song of Solomon 1:6). The silent moderate majority has kept silent; there has been a lack of broader church discipline for the sake of the movement and it has not gone unnoticed by outsiders. Let's speak up and let's start by "setting our own house in order."

Let me finish with a few suggestions on how the moderate majority could deal with these issues. What do I mean about "speaking up"? I mean speak the truth in love and leave the fallout to our sovereign God.

1. We should publically exhort, censure, and if needed, discipline those who act uncharitably against a brother and engage in behaviour unbecoming of the gospel.
2. We should be more concerned about truth and honesty than we are about our movements, organizations, and institutions. Is it not ironic that fundamentalists have become guilty of

---

[86] http://www.biblicalevangelist.org/jack_hyles_chapter3.php; accessed August 19, 2015.

what Mr. Spurgeon said concerning liberals in his day? They "subordinate the maintenance of truth to denominational prosperity and unity."[87]

3. We should engage in instructive and intelligent writing that deals with aberrations in theology and Christian practice, whether liberal, ecumenical, or fundamentalist. Negative sound bytes on social media, nitpicking, and theological rants are more harmful than helpful.

4. We should be willing to discuss issues and differences with meekness and seek to understand brethren who hold the same principles but differ in practice. The issues facing the church today are not the same as the liberal/fundamentalist controversy of years past.

---

[87] Arnold Dallimore, *Spurgeon: A New Biography* (Edinburgh: Banner of Truth Trust, 1995), 207.

FUNDAMENTALISM AND THE NEW CONSERVATIVE EVANGELICALISM IDENTITY

In the preceding chapters I have tried to address some of the problems with fundamentalism. I have not been—nor should anyone be—afraid to face these hard issues head-on, to admit the difficulties, and to attempt to correct them. Five of the seven churches in Asia Minor had rebuke-worthy faults mingled with virtues in Revelation 2 and 3. The task that the Lord burdened those churches with is the same task that we are burdened with: to recognize our corporate faults and correct them. Failure to do this will only compound our sin.

In analyzing fundamentalism, however, it has not been my intention either to take potshots at or to trash the whole movement. I am not about to join the band of evangelicals among whom it "has become fashionable...to join in criticism of fundamentalism," as Iain Murray puts it.[88] Those who do so reveal their own narrow prejudice, identify themselves with other movements with similar faults, and forget that fundamentalism is indeed part of the church of Christ. They may in

---

[88] Murray, *John MacArthur*, 59.

fact be guilty of what W. H. Griffith Thomas accused B. B. Warfield of when Warfield criticized the Keswick movement:

> "the absence of any recognition of the fact that the movement he criticizes and condemns expresses a spiritual experience and not merely a theological theory."[89]

Over the years there has been some traffic between fundamentalism and the broader evangelical church. Some have left fundamentalism for other groups and some have come into the fundamentalist fold. Of those, some have studied at fundamentalist colleges and universities for an education or for a conservative experience they could not get elsewhere.

In recent years, however, the landscape of evangelical Christianity in North America has changed considerably. The gap between fundamentalism and conservative evangelicalism is narrowing and a new conservative evangelical identity is beginning to emerge. The defection from fundamentalism continues despite the fact that there is a definite corrective among many fundamentalist leaders—most notable in Bob Jones University. In addition to this, there is a growing tension in the broader evangelical church creating a more conservative right-wing evangelicalism that one writer has identified as a "resurgent fundamentalism."[90]

Consider, first, the current defection from fundamentalism. The past ten years have witnessed a sharp increase in defections from fundamentalism. Some of them can be chalked up to the general

---

89 Cited in Marsden, *Fundamentalism and American Culture*, 99.
90 Roger E. Olson, cited in *Four Views on The Spectrum of Evangelicalism*, eds. Naselli and Hansen, 52.

malaise of the church and the trend toward secularization in the West. Much of the bleeding of fundamentalism, however, has been precipitated by the awareness that there are other ways—and better ways—to be a fundamentalist.

Some believe that those who leave fundamentalism do it because they have a rebellious spirit or a desire to lower the standards. Many young defectors have been accused of that. On the contrary, some who leave the fundamentalist movement do so as a result of growth in grace and the leading of the Lord, and often at great personal sacrifice.

Some leave because they have been damaged by the bloody "war psychology" and the infighting that characterized the movement. They are still hurting from the "fundamentalism back then [that] was cruel and unbiblical…and so cannibalistic," to use the words of John MacArthur.[91]

In addition, many are coming to the realization that the doctrine of separation was over-emphasized, misinformed, and sometimes abused to the point that it implied that outside fundamentalism there is no salvation. In speaking of those in other churches, the word "apostate" was used too often and too freely. Young fundamentalists now have access to the teaching ministries of other evangelicals and they see no correlation between what they are hearing and reading of these men and what they were told by their fundamentalist leaders. With access to all of the data, the millennial generation has been exposed to a broader church and many have been surprised to discover that outside their fundamentalist boundaries there are—and there have been for many years—others standing for the truth of the gospel and the fundamentals of the faith!

---

91 http://www.christianpost.com/news/macarthur-tells-christians-don-t-fornicate-with-the-world-44114/; accessed October 14, 2015.

These errors in the movement continued uncorrected for too long and this has undermined the trust of many. Many feel that fundamentalism demanded only one thing from them: cooperation. It required that they conform to a set standard of values that robbed the individual of his individuality and impeded the Christian's right and duty to personal and individual growth in grace. This has left many young fundamentalists spiritually stunted, struggling, and angry on the inside, while they have gone on for years conforming to an inconsistent and demoralizing legalism. We need to acknowledge this. Some of the older generation are willing to own the mistakes and to initiate correctives. Others are not so willing, and concerns and correctives are met with a stone wall and a parapet of protection from which the old-guard launch their attacks and maintain the old standards. Many of the youth, who admit that the winds of change are beginning to blow, are not willing to wait for the changes to take effect. For them, it is too little, too late.

Furthermore, the revival of Reformed theology in the later part of the last century paved the way for change and provided an attractive and biblical alternative. Young Christians growing up in conservative churches are feeding on conservative writers and, because fundamentalists have not been writing, they are reading the only available material from Reformed writers—Martin Lloyd-Jones, A. W. Pink, John MacArthur, John Piper, R. C. Sproul, etc., not to mention the Puritan authors now available. As a result, young men are entering fundamentalist colleges already conversant with Reformed theology and this is having a huge impact on the Arminian fundamentalist ethos.

Consider, second, the shift among fundamentalist leaders. Many of the current leaders in fundamentalism recognize the sincerity of heart in the defectors and are working hard to correct the ills and staunch the bleeding. Many have moderated their positions and have laboured for a more palatable presentation and defense of the faith.

This is not a small thing for fundamentalists. It is nothing short of a paradigm shift and they ought to be commended for their foresight and courage. In some cases, it comes at a cost. I mentioned previously the ACCC's attack on one of its own, Kevin Bauder. More recently, Steve Pettit, the new president of Bob Jones University has come under attack from a one-time ally, H. T. Spence of Foundations Bible College in North Carolina. Bauder and Pettit, among others, acknowledge the corporate fault and recognize that some of the methods and manners of the past were misplaced, over-emphasized, and, in some cases, downright wrong. Old walls are being torn down, reconciliation is being made where individuals were wronged, new friendships are being forged, and there is a desire to revisit the texts of Scripture on many of the issues.

This shift, then, is not a denial of the historic faith or a desire to be seeker sensitive. It is not a departure from the core principles of fundamentalism but a correction of the "capital mistake" pointed out by J. E. Carnell; it is a return to the classic creeds of the church. It is an honest desire on the part of right-thinking Christians to recognize the church of Christ in its historical context—a church beyond themselves, a church less sectarian and more catholic, a church that attempts to engage the culture without losing the gospel.

Finally, consider the new conservative evangelical identity. Many who leave fundamentalism try to distance themselves from the movement and go to the other extreme. Others are more cautious in leaving the chilly climate of fundamentalism for the warm, inviting atmosphere of conservative evangelicalism. They might be surprised to discover that conservative evangelicals are not the enemy at the gate and they have more affinity with fundamentalism than they might have expected.

In conservative evangelicalism, they are going to meet people who have, we might say, the DNA of a fundamentalist: the same standards of personal holiness, the same high view of Scripture, and also, surprisingly, a clear biblical criteria for separation—though perhaps applied a little differently. In short, they will discover that many parts of the broader evangelical church do not subscribe to the principles laid out by the older new evangelicalism—a term which some fundamentalists still insist on using as a catch-all for non-fundamentalists.

They are going to meet those who admire the fundamentalist for the courage of his conviction, for the strength he has to stand at the cost of personal reputation. They are going to be challenged to be gracious and to not take pot shots at fundamentalism, as they were admonished by John Piper at his 2008 Desiring God Conference.[92]

They are also going to discover that conservative evangelicals have been fighting furiously in recent years for some important doctrines of the church: lordship salvation and inerrancy, for example. They have been strong and unrelenting against Open Theism, the Charismatic movement, gender confusion, and Evangelicals and Catholics Together (ECT). It is conservative evangelicals, not the fundamentalists, who are now getting the reputation for militancy.

The courage of many of these conservative evangelicals has gained them favour among many fundamentalists and distinguished them

---

92 John Piper, "20 Reasons I Don't Take Potshots at Fundamentalists" (Desiring God blog, June 2, 2008); http://www.desiringgod.org/articles/20-reasons-i-dont-take-potshots-at-fundamentalists; accessed April 18, 2016.

from more left-wing evangelicals so that this has even been referred to as *resurgent fundamentalism.*

The more right-wing (hyper) fundamentalists may call this a shift into *pseudo-fundamentalism* or *neo-fundamentalism.* These terms have gained no traction and probably will not do so. Remnants of the mood and mentality of historic (militant) fundamentalism lingers in a few isolated churches, colleges, and in certain individuals. Many of these have recognized the sentence of death on the movement and are labouring hard to shore up the old belligerence and to maintain the so-called "old paths" (a biblical phrase often misused; see Jeremiah 6:16). The same old war psychology lingers. Every now and again we hear the rattle of sabres, but it has more the tones of a death rattle than the sound of a serious or effective charge of war.

The hyper-fundamentalists will continue to make peripheral issues a reason for separation and to defend their position with arguments that lean more on Christian values than on the text of Scripture. They will find themselves more and more marginalized, lonely, and isolated from the onward march of the church of Christ and will find comfort only in the martyr spirit of the proverbial remnant—as though they alone are the chosen of God.

A WAY FORWARD

"The idea of fundamentalism," Kevin Bauder says "is a great idea. It is a necessary idea. More importantly, it is a biblical idea.... Some version of fundamentalism is necessary." However, he continues,

> it needs to be chastened fundamentalism. It needs to become even more serious about worship, preaching, devotion, and holiness. It needs to become more doctrinally careful. It desperately needs to distance itself from the excesses of its worst exemplars.[93]

I believe, as I stated in the introduction, that fundamentalism is a biblical idea. This is what our forefather's fought for. The fundamentalism of the 1920s and 30s was theologically focused, it was purely a defense of the faith. It was not things *connected* to the faith, or *subservient* to the faith, or *subsequent* to the faith but "the faith"—it was a fight for biblical Christianity. Even liberals have admitted this much. Kirsopp Lake stated in 1925,

> It is a mistake often made by educated persons who happen to have but little knowledge of historical

---

93 Bauder, "Fundamentalism" in *Four Views on The Spectrum of Evangelicalism*, eds. Naselli and Hansen, 47.

theology to suppose that fundamentalism is a new and strange form of thought.[94]

I have a friend, a member of my congregation, who first heard the word fundamentalist from his high-school teacher in a private Christian School, not too long ago. As he defended the historical accuracy of the Old Testament stories, the teacher dismissed him with, "Oh you're one of those fundamentalists." My friend went home and looked up the name that he had been called and discovered that he is indeed a fundamentalist—he believes the Bible to be the Word of God.

Kirsopp Lake, and my friend's high-school teacher were speaking, of course, about what we might call *theological fundamentalism* before it developed all of the political and cultural phenomena, and the theological eccentricities that we see today—the "excesses and vagaries" that we heard about from Beale and the "unscriptural behavior" that Pickering and others have spoken about.[95]

So how can we get back to the historic fundamentalism? How can we return to a fundamentalism that is gospel oriented, where separation is practiced but not predominant? How can we return to a fundamentalism that is focused, not on separation, but on the gospel to which we are all separated?[96] How can we return to a

---

94 Kirsopp Lake, *The Religion of Yesterday and Tomorrow* (Boston: Houghton, 1926), 61.
95 See also Beale, *In Pursuit of Purity*; Burggraff, "Fundamentalism at the End of the Twentieth Century," 25; Ernest Pickering, *The Tragedy of Compromise: The Origin and Impact of the New Evangelicalism* (Greenville: Bob Jones University Press, 1994), 8. Also, John Ashbrook wrote his *Axioms of Fundamentalism* with the hope that "some beleaguered young fundamentalist…may be encouraged that they are on the right road," *The Revivalist* (February 1976): 1–3. In part, the World Congress of Fundamentalists convened in 1976 to correct some of the fractioning of the movement.
96 Romans 1:1.

fundamentalism that is militant but where militancy does not set the mood or create the atmosphere? This is possible. This is biblical. This is the way forward.[97]

First, we need to own our faults. Some fundamentalists have deflected the criticism by saying, "It's not just the fundamentalists who act unscripturally. What about the Reformed movement?" This is true. Other movements and organizations have their problems. However, deflecting criticism does not deal with the long-standing problems within fundamentalism, rather, it compounds the problem rather than corrects it.

Others have tried to excuse unscriptural behaviour by a flippant admission that even the fundamentalists are totally depraved, or as Ernest Pickering put it, "fundamentalists have demonstrated amply the fact that they also have 'old natures.'"[98] These generalizations might go some way to *explaining* the problems, but they should never be used to *excuse* the sins of the movement. Surely the gospel that we have expended so much energy defending should deliver us from this depravity, not excuse it. A gospel that is not effective and evident in our lives is not worth defending.

Second, we need a biblical identity. As I said previously, there have been many attempts to correct the destructive fighting spirit of fundamentalism: the harsh condemnations and *ad homonym* attacks,

---

[97] See the four suggestions on pages 85-86. See also, Kevin Bauder, "A Fundamentalism Worth Saving"; http://www.aaccs.info/media/Bauder%20A%20Fundamentalism%20Worth%20Savin g.pdf; accessed May 13, 2016.

[98] Pickering, *The Tragedy of Compromise*, 8.

and the militant, aggressive, and indiscriminate separation.[99] The most obvious corrective, of course, was the New Evangelicals in the late 1940s. The New Evangelicals however went to the other extreme of undiscerning love and acceptance. One extreme is as problematic as the other.

Despite sincere attempts, however, to better the situation, there has been little advance and failure to achieve corrections has precipitated the decline of fundamentalism.

The problem lies, I believe, in the fact that fundamentalism, motivated by a love for the truth, identified itself as a militant movement, a fighting machine against error. This became its reason for existence. "The only true fundamentalist" says Beale, "is a fighting fundamentalist."[100] According this measure, holding to the fundamentals of the faith is not sufficient in order for one to be counted faithful. This is how many understood these sentiments.

Those within the movement saw themselves only as soldiers, the military police of the church. Local churches became mess halls, barracks and rallying points. This self-identity obligated the fundamentalist to unrelenting and indiscriminate fighting and to militant activism. People saved into this army—for there was a great deal of evangelism going on—were handed a placard to protest before they had learned the basics of the Christian religion or the fundamentals of the faith they were to defend.

---

99 The World Congress of Fundamentalists was formed with the distinct purpose of correcting the tendency to "fractionalize and divide" caused by the "militancy" of Fundamentalism. *The Revivalist* (February 1976): front page.
100 Beale, *In Pursuit of Purity*, 357.

In this atmosphere, "bearing reproach" (Hebrews 13:13) became a badge of honour and a seal of success—notwithstanding that the reproach was often precipitated by foolish excesses. The children of fundamentalists learned to "bear reproach" for the sake of their parents or their fundamentalist leaders and grew into adulthood thinking that if they were not "bearing reproach" they were not being *faithful* to the cause of Christ. Christianity was bound up in this identity, and the "battle scars" were the Christian's "best credentials."[101]

This type of fundamentalism was led by those of a particular emotional temperament, those who possessed a more robust disposition. Those who did not own this temperament joined the ranks of the "silent moderate majority" and enjoyed watching it, others tolerated it, while still others—weary of the militant activism—found more accommodating surroundings.

Fundamentalist leaders and authors have recognized this tendency to weariness and refer to it often. They speak of those who have "grow[n] weary of the battle."[102] Many have been described as being "disheartened"[103] and beleaguered."[104] They have been accused of betraying and stabbing their brethren in the back.[105] They have been slighted as those who have paid no price of suffering and of "taking for granted the truths for which the fathers had to fight."[106] These are

---

101 Ian R. K. Paisley, *The Revivalist* (January 1983): 4. The title of a sermon preached by Dr. Paisley in the Martyrs Memorial Free Presbyterian Church, Belfast, Northern Ireland, on August 1, 1982.

102 Pickering, *The Tragedy of Compromise*, 6.

103 Pickering, *The Tragedy of Compromise*, 7

104 John Ashbrook, *Axioms of Separation* (Ohio: Here I Stand Books, n.d.), 3.

105 Jones, *Cornbread and Caviar*, 171.

106 Beale, *In Pursuit of Purity*, 357.

a few of the unwarranted accusations that have been levelled against those who leave fundamentalism.

Did it never occur to the "fighting fundamentalist" that the burden of battle to which he obligates both himself and others, is emotionally, physically and spiritually exhausting. For many, it is a burden too heavy to bear (Matthew 23:4). Perhaps it is the same weariness that Martha felt when she complained to the Lord Jesus because her sister did not serve (Luke 10:38–42).

The sense of oppression came because the "fighting fundamentalist" created an atmosphere where it seemed they were always fighting *for* the victory and never *in* the victory, never enjoying the victory that overcomes (1 John 5:4). It seemed they were always defending the faith rather than enjoying it. The church was a perpetual battlefield when it should also have been a *schoolroom* to teach, a *hospital ward* to heal, a *counselling room* to guide and encourage, and a *home* free from the fear of criticism and strife where one could sit at the feet of Jesus and be fed.

Until the fundamentalist redefines himself in more general terms— that includes more than militancy and separation—he will go on fighting. Until he breaks from the ball and chain of unrelenting and indiscriminate militancy he will go on searching for error and inconsistencies among his brethren—because he has obligated himself to such a fight. If fundamentalist churches are to survive, reach out to a lost and dying world and be an attraction to other believers, they will have to find a biblical identity, they will have to return to the old paths of good old-fashioned Christian love, which characterized the early church.

Loving as Jesus loves does not exclude contending for the faith nor deny separation from error. Loving as Jesus loves is demanding on the flesh. It intrudes into our comfort zone, searches our hearts and humbles us. Love is not suspicious nor selfish, but magnanimous and self-sacrificing. Love has opinions but is not opinionated; it judges but is not judgmental, it is discerning but it accepts diversity with patience (1 Corinthians 13:4-6). This is a work of grace (Romans 5:5) and a fruit of the Spirit (Galatians 5:22-23). This love, that loves even the enemy, as Tertullian said, is "peculiar to Christians alone."[107] This should be our identity, our distinctive characteristic, and our witness to the world, as Jesus Himself said, "by *this* shall all men know that ye are my disciples, if ye have love one to another" (John 13:35, emphasis added).

Third, we need to learn to be "angry and sin not" (Ephesians 4:26). Love and anger are not incompatible emotions; indeed anger often arises out of love. George Marsden famously described a fundamentalist as "an evangelical who is angry about something."[108] Marsden's definition is flawed of course, if it does not allow for "righteous anger." But I would suggest that the fundamentalist that Marsden is describing is one whose anger is indiscriminate, undiscerning and unrestrained. John Newton wrote,

> All religious parties profess a great regard to the precept, Jude 3. "Contend earnestly for the faith." And if noisy anger, bold assertions, harsh censures, and bitter persecuting zeal, can singly or jointly answer the apostle's design, there is hardly a party but may glory in their obedience. But if the weapons of our warfare are not carnal; if the wrath of man worketh not the

---

107 Tertullian, "To Scapula" in *The Anti-Nicene Fathers* (Peabody: Hendrickson Publications, 2004) 3:105.

108 George M. Marsden, *Understanding Fundamentalism and Evangelicalism* (Grand Rapids: William B. Eerdmans Publishing Company, 1991), 1.

righteousness of God; if the true Christian contention can only be maintained by Scripture arguments, meekness, patience, prayer, and an exemplary conversion—if this is the true state of the case, where is the Church party (may I not say, where is the person) that has not still much to learn and to practice in this point?[109]

For many fundamentalists, irenic (peaceful) fundamentalism is not an option; indeed, some would say that irenic fundamentalism is incompatible with the Bible—as one colleague and brother put it to me: "'Irenic fundamentalists?' What are those? You seem to be advocating for non-militant fundamentalism, ie, no fundamentalism at all" [sic].

This is exactly what I am advocating for: *irenic fundamentalism*. A fundamentalism that can contend without being contentious and be militant without being clamorous; a fundamentalism that seeks peace and pursues it (Psalm 34:14); a fundamentalism that can do battle, but whose battle cry is love: "to love the captive soul, but to rage against the captor."[110]

Fundamentalists, of course, do not have a monopoly on anger or strife. The disciples struggled with it (Mark 14:47). On his deathbed, John Calvin acknowledged those who had "borne patiently with [his] vehemence, which was sometimes carried to excess."[111] Eight times in his letters, the apostle Paul provides a list of vices that are common

---

109 John Newton, *The Works of John Newton*, 4 vol. (Edinburgh: Banner of Truth Trust, 1988) 3:237.

110 Keith Getty and Stuart Townend, "O Church Arise," in *Hymns Modern and Ancient* (Milwaukee: Heart Publications, 2011), No. 95.

111 Theodore Beza, *Life of Calvin*, in *Tracks and Letters of John Calvin*, 7 vol. (Edinburgh: Banner of Truth Trust, 2009), 1:xc.

dangers in the church of Christ (Romans 1:29; 1 Corinthians 5:11; 6:9–10; 2 Corinthians 12:20; Galatians 5:19; Ephesians 4:31; 5:3; Colossians 3:5). Two of these lists relate only to sexual immorality (Ephesians 5:3; Colossians 3:5). All of the other catalogues of sins include anger, wrath, emulation, spite, malice, strife, outbursts, clamoring, etc.

There are two categories of anger: holy, or righteous anger, and unholy anger. Holy anger is a God-given resistance to all that dishonours God and hinders the greater good of God's people. This is a God-honouring response. Thomas Boston defines righteous anger as,

> a commotion of the spirit, arising from the apprehension of a real sinful evil, with hatred of it, grief for it, and a desire of the vindication of the right and honor of the injured, for the destruction of sin.[112]

A Christian should be angry over sin, error, and anything that encroaches on the glory of God and the wellbeing of his church. Anger is a Christian emotion. Perhaps the problem with the New Evangelicals was they weren't angry enough. We know from personal experience, however, that uncontrolled anger is damaging and can paralyze any attempt to move forward. In many respects, this is what has happened in fundamentalism. There was a focus on what makes us angry (the enemies and the errors) and we have been reactionary, impulsive, and busy trying to destroy what only Christ can—and has—destroyed.

For the fundamentalist, very often those with whom he disagrees have set the agenda, and the movement has been distracted from the calm

---

112 Thomas Boston, *Complete Works of Thomas Boston*, 12 vol. (1853, reprint; Lafayette: Sovereign Grace Publishers, 2001) 4:353.

and purposeful work of the church, "for the perfecting of the saints, for the work of the ministry, for the edifying of the body of Christ" (Ephesians 4:12).

Consider the life of the Lord Jesus, our great Exemplar. He came with a mission to accomplish and he fulfilled his purpose. It is true that the Lord Jesus overturned tables in the Temple in a manifest state of anger and he railed against the Scribes and Pharisees. But these occasions did not characterize his ministry, nor hinder his purpose. There were also times when Jesus was angry and said nothing (Mark 3:5). He was effectively resisting evil simply by his action to the contrary, by setting a positive example, to the chagrin and defeat of those who opposed him. This is irenic Christianity. This is the way forward.

Fourth, Fundamentalists need to promote biblical discernment. Fundamentalists need to distinguish between theological heresy and theological inconsistency, between essentials and non-essentials. As self-identified "contenders," fundamentalists obligated themselves to "expose and oppose" error. This was initially directed toward liberals when liberalism was the obvious enemy. As time went by however, and liberalism was no longer in the crosshairs, many fundamentalists directed their anger at other evangelicals, and at times toward others within fundamentalism.

Their guns were now directed, not toward those who *denied* the gospel but toward those whom the fundamentalist deemed were *undermining* the gospel. Two problems became evident in these evangelical skirmishes. First, there was a failure to recognize the nuances of theological discussion and different applications of the same principles. Second, battles were fought over Bible versions, contemporary Christian music, separation, etc., with the same vehemence as that which was expressed against the liberal—there was no distinction made. Fundamentalism created a Christian culture that was too black and white, too simplistic, and that demanded of secondary issues (matters of indifference) the same loyalty as primary issues.

Furthermore, because there was no discernment in the issues, many fundamentalists were willing to stir up strife against anyone in the name of "the defense of the faith." They dredged through the life and ministry of other evangelicals searching for material to fight about—"exposing and opposing" in the name of the gospel. In this indiscriminate fight, fundamentalists failed to realize that their militant activism was undermining the gospel they were attempting to defend—and the moderate majority watched in silence, often cringing in horror.

Biblical Christianity calls for a higher standard, for deeper thinking, and for greater grace—as a testimony toward those outside the church (1 Thessalonians 4:12). In the complexities of life in a fallen world, biblical Christianity anticipates hard choices and difficult people and therefore demands grace and spiritual discernment. Furthermore, it requires each person to stand with his own conscience before God (Romans 14:4).

At the beginning of his epistle to the Philippians, Paul prays that their love might "abound more and more in knowledge and in all judgement." Philippians 1:9–11 reads,

> And this I pray, that your love may abound yet more and more in knowledge and in all judgment; that ye may approve things that are excellent; that ye may be sincere and without offence till the day of Christ. Being filled with the fruits of righteousness, which are by Jesus Christ, unto the glory and praise of God.

The English translation struggles to convey the depth of meaning conveyed in Paul's prayer. The word *judgement* (verse 9) is translated in other versions as *discernment* (NASB, RSV, ESV and ASV) and has the idea of perception, intuitive insight, or a sense. This word is found nowhere else in the New Testament. However, the word *senses* found in Hebrews 5:14 is related and helps us understand its meaning. Hebrews 5:14 reads, "But strong meat belongeth to them that are of full age, even those who by reason of use have their senses exercised to discern both good and evil." In the original Greek, the word *senses* is the word from which we get our English word *aesthetic*, meaning that which has a sense of beauty. We don't go to school to learn what is aesthetically pleasing. We know this by our daily interaction with the world around us. Therefore, the spiritual discernment that Paul is praying for is not learned by books but is acquired by our interaction with the Word of God and prayer.

This discernment, Paul says, has a purpose, that we might be able to "try those things that differ" (lit.), and thereby, as most translations render it, "approve those things that are excellent." To paraphrase, Paul is praying that the Philippians would manifest a loving discernment, so that they may be able to make spiritually informed choices in matters of indifference, choose the excellent thing, and avoid offense.

Evidently Paul recognized that *sound* doctrine and practice could be maintained by *unsound* methods, and the work of the kingdom, the defence of the faith, is not a mere intellectual fight. He knows it is a spiritual fight against "principalities and powers" that requires spiritual insight. He prayed, therefore, that beyond the clear statements of Scripture (the fundamentals) there may be the "spirit of wisdom" in their application of Scripture and the Philippians would have insight into the *best way*, the *best choice*, the *best word* in a given situation, in order that they might not give offense (Philippians 1:9–10).

Intelligence might choose between *good* and *bad*, but only godly and loving spiritual discernment can choose between what is *good* and what is *best*. "This" says Richard Lenski "is masterly thinking."[113] This is the way forward.

Finally, we need rethink biblical militancy. Fundamentalism too often took its principle of militancy from the New Testament and its model of fighting from the Old Testament. Fundamentalists too often forgot that the story of David and Goliath is about Christ, not about our aggression, our cause, our fight. They forgot that David defeated the giant and the Israelites routed the enemy. Christians are like the Israelites chasing the already defeated enemy, not David destroying Goliath. There is cause, but Christ has taken up that cause. Christians follow in his train; we fight in his victory.

Don't misunderstand me, I believe that we have a fight to fight, a cause to maintain; but fundamentalism has been such a fight-driven movement that it often overlooked the primary meaning of Scripture to get to a particular application. This over emphasis impinged on a Christ-centered ministry, threatened the spiritual life of the church, and failed to lay a strong foundation for a coming generation ill prepared for the new battles facing the church today. The sword of battle was disproportionate to the use of the trowel in building (Nehemiah 4:15–17).

---

113 Richard C. H. Lenski, *An Interpretation of St. Paul's Epistles to the Galatians, to the Ephesians, and to the Philippians* (1937, reprint; Peabody: Hendrickson Publications, 2001), 718.

In the late 1880s, Charles Spurgeon took up the fight against liberalism in the Baptist Union of Great Britain and Ireland. Arnold Dallimore states that "Spurgeon's attitude towards the situation was immediately one of militant opposition."[114] At the height of that controversy Spurgeon wrote, "The sword and trowel have both been used this year with all our might. We have built up the wall of the city, and we have tried to smite the King's enemies."[115] His biographer wrote that he was "most effective in opposing error when he simply proclaimed the truth."[116]

Of all of the books of the New Testament, the little epistle of Jude has been used as the manual for militant activism. Jude's first choice of subject was the "common salvation," but conditions in the church were such that demanded immediate attention. The bulk of the epistle is taken up with identifying the apostates throughout history. Jude, however, does not outline any strategy for attack or any methodology for active combat because "we wrestle not against flesh and blood" (Ephesians 6:12).

Notice how Jude addresses his subject. Apart from the introductory greeting (verses 1–2) and the concluding doxology (verses 24–25), there are three main divisions that are clearly identified in Jude's letter. First, Jude recognizes a problem that had arisen in the church (verses 3–4) and that still exists: there are "certain men" who are a danger to the body of Christ (verse 4). The men are referred to repeatedly by the demonstrative pronoun "these" (verses 8, 10, 12, 16, 19). Jude is dealing with what Peter had previously prophesied would take place (2 Peter 2:1; 3:3). There is a very definite and immediate

---

114 Dallimore, *Spurgeon*, 205.

115 C. H. Spurgeon, *The "Down Grade" Controversy* (Pasadena: Pilgrim Publications, n.d.), 3.

116 G. Holden Pike, *The Life and Work of Charles Haddon Spurgeon*, 6 vol. (1894, reprint; Edinburgh: Banner of Truth Trust, 1991) 5:265.

danger of libertines creeping into the church, manifesting themselves by their theological heresy (verse 4), moral impurity (verses 4, 10, 16, 18), and spiritual bankruptcy (verse 12-13, 19). Notice the danger is not just theological error!

Second, Jude shows us that this problem is not a new one. This spirit of rebellion has a long history in the church (verses 5-19). Indeed, it goes back before the creation of man when the angels sinned against the grace of heaven. He mentions Israel also, who sinned against the grace of the covenant, and the Sodomites, who sinned against the grace of nature and conscience (verses 5-7). Jude uses the greater part of the letter to convince his readers this is not new and it should not take us by surprise. We ought not to consider these issues in the church, then, as a threat to the *foundation* of the church but more as "pests" disrupting the *function* of the church. Jude has already assured the believers that they are *sanctified, preserved,* and *called* (verses 1-2) and he concludes with the assurance that the sovereign God is able to "keep you from falling" (verse 24). In the providence of God then, these infiltrators are intended to keep us attentive to our own spiritual vitality.

This brings us to the heart of Jude's message. The third point that Jude makes is that the church has a duty to deal with the problem. We must "earnestly contend for the faith" (verse 3). In verses 20-23, Jude returns to the exhortation of contending by outlining for us *how* we are to do this. The insidious infiltration of ungodly men into the church ought to have a sanctifying influence rather than embitter us. These problems and threats in the church should keep us founded on the Word of truth (verse 17), fascinated with grace of Christ (verses 20-21), and disciplined in how we react to the world around us (verses 22-23).

The book of Jude, therefore, is as much a reminder and a challenge to the church as it is an exposé of apostasy. Jude makes it clear that contending has more to do with ourselves and the struggle for our own spiritual vitality than it has to do with our denunciations of heresy and protests against those outside the church.

> The major way to resist doctrinal and moral error is to put into practice the admonitions of verses 20–23, in particular those of verses 20–21…. It is in verses 20–21 that Jude prescribes the antidote to error: "Beloved, building yourselves up on your most holy faith; praying in the Holy Spirit, keep yourselves in the love of God, looking for the mercy of our Lord Jesus Christ unto eternal life."[117]

---

117 Michael A. G. Haykin, *The Empire of the Holy Spirit* (Mountain Home: BorderStone Press, 2010), 70.

APPENDIX:

UNDERSTANDING THE POWERFUL
PERSONALITIES OF FUNDAMENTALISM

On Easter Sunday evening in 1990, when I was a zealous seventeen year old, a few friends and I made the fifteen minute drive to a more informal after-meeting for the youth in Dr. Ian Paisley's church in east Belfast, Northern Ireland. That was a big year for us young fundamentalists. In July, the World Congress of Christian Fundamentalists would meet in London, England, and I was planning to attend, along with hundreds of fundamentalists who would converge from around the world to celebrate their orthodoxy.

At Paisley's annual Easter Convention, however, a sampling of fundamentalists gathered from the United Kingdom and the U.S.A. The event, after the Easter Sunday evening service, was a question and answer session, something like the Jewish practice of sitting at the feet of the rabbis, listening to them and asking them questions.

One of the questions that evening had to do with fundamentalism, in particular the distinction between first- and second-generation fundamentalists. I remember two things about Paisley's answer. The first thing was a little humorous and awkward—at least I thought so—

for one man. Paisley implied that this man was a "second-generation" fundamentalist while he believed himself to be a "first-generation" fundamentalist. Paisley attempted to show that "first-generation" status was obviously a badge to be worn with pride.

The second thing I remember about that evening was the emphasis that Paisley put on the need for young people to know the history of fundamentalism and the sacrifice it had taken to be a first–generation fundamentalist. He emphasized the cost and the sacrifice that first-generation fundamentalists had to make. This application to us young people was a regular occurrence when Paisley was on the subject. Preaching in 1981 at the thirtieth anniversary of the first Free Presbyterian Church in Crossgar, Paisley said,

> I would say to the young people here…we are leaving you a great heritage. Be faithful to it! Remember the sacrifices that were made that you might have a church free from apostasy and popery, and free to serve the Lord Christ. [118]

Paisley was correct when he said that they left a "great heritage." That heritage is the gospel, the Reformed faith (in the Northern Ireland context at least). For that, we salute them. But that heritage was not without its problems; it was, in some respects, a poisoned chalice. It is this that has occupied the public conversation of fundamentalists now for a couple of decades.

Ironically, the character traits needed to build and defend the walls of fundamentalism were the same as those that did so much harm within the walls. Dealing with the lives and legacy of some of these leaders is not easy. Some of the things that went on and the things

---

[118] Ian R. K. Paisley in *The Revivalist* (May 1981): 11.

that were said are shocking. Some can be chalked up to pulpit rhetoric, and others, while inexcusable, can be explained in their context. We need to try to work our way through this maze. We may not get through to the end, but I hope we will get set in the right direction.

The legacy that many of these men left was not as endearing as they might have hoped and some of it has already been recorded in these pages. Arnold Dallimore, who held T. T. Shields in very high regard, concluded his biography of Shields with these striking words:

> Had he overcome these faults and really lived for the glory of God, as he supposed he was doing, his name would have wrung [sic] with splendour among Christians today, instead of being so sadly forgotten as it is now. [119]

One prominent characteristic of these men was the overwhelming sense of divine destiny they had and what appeared to be, and perhaps was, an inordinate pride. It was this belief—that they were called of God and were fulfilling God's purpose—that governed everything they did, enabled them to plough through every difficulty, and rise above every criticism.

These men viewed themselves in this calling as "the Lord's anointed" (1 Chronicles 16:22) and sometimes used the language of the Old Testament in this regard. Anyone who spoke against them was speaking against the purpose of God and could therefore—and indeed should be—condemned for doing so. One colleague of Shields' for example, who disagreed with him in the late 1940s, was labelled an

---

[119] Arnold Dallimore, "Thomas Todhunter Shields: Baptist Fundamentalist" (unpublished manuscript, n.d.).

"Absalom" and a "Judas"—caustic language to use to refer to another minster of the gospel who was also the "Lord's anointed"![120]

In 2012 when Nancy Anderson finished her biography of Carl McIntire, she sent me a copy—for which I thank her. One of the first things I looked for in the book was to see whether she had addressed the personality flaws that were so evident in McIntire's life. I was pleased to see that she did, not because of any malice towards McIntire, but simply in the interests of honest biography. Anderson identified McIntire's need to control: "some called him 'Dictator' or 'Pope.'" She quoted Joel Belz,

> Nearly everyone who worked with McIntire eventually became disillusioned, and McIntire himself, who had separated from denominations throughout his life, in the end, separated from his friends. [121]

Anderson continued, "Carl saw himself destined by God to lead this great movement."[122]

The same sense of destiny was in T. T. Shields of Toronto and Ian Paisley of Belfast. Arnold Dallimore said of Shields that "he carried with him throughout his career a constant awareness of his greatness."[123] Paisley was very much the same. He frequently portrayed himself as the repition of a great leader, whether in religion or in politics. In the church, he saw himself as a Moses leading the

---

[120] *The Gospel Witness* (January 27, 1949): 3–8; *The Gospel Witness* (October 27, 1949): 9.

[121] Joel Belz, "This Fight's Over: Lessons From a Fiery Fundamentalist," in *World* (April 6, 2002): 5. Cited in Gladys Titzck Rhoads and Nancy Titzck Anderson, *McIntire: Defender of Faith and Freedom* (Maitland: Xulon Press, 2012), 514.

[122] Rhoads and Anderson, *McIntire*, 514.

[123] Dallimore, "Thomas Todhunter Shields: Baptist Fundamentalist."

people out of captivity and believed that upon his death, the Lord would raise up a Joshua to lead them into the Promised Land. This is what Paisley told John Hume, a former political leader and opponent, who chided him with the hope that the church would close when Paisley died.[124]

In politics it was similar. In 1981 Paisley led a political crusade right across the country. The route he took was the same route that Sir Edward Carson took in 1911, ending with a great political rally in Belfast's Ulster Hall. Paisley called it "The Carson Trail." Indeed, he was hoisted up to the level of the Carson statue on the grounds of the Stormont Estate (the parliament of Northern Ireland) and got his picture taken in the same posture as Ulster's great hero.

We should remember that these men were indeed great men, but they were only men with feet of clay. Many on the outside look at them with only disdain and condemnation. Their view is ill-informed and wrong. Many on the inside have the same view, unfortunately, and they also are ill-informed, imbalanced, and ungracious. Others recognize that although these leaders had their faults—sometimes deep, glaring, and ugly—yet they were men whose lives were anchored in an unshakable faith and an intense love for God and his gospel. Perhaps a greater share of the blame should go to those who blindly followed, encouraged, or stood back and tolerated the excesses. Very often the image of a public figure can be propped up and magnified by those around him.

It should be said, however, in the interests of honesty that much of what I have dealt with as far as the characteristics of fundamentalism—the tendency towards legalism, a harsh, and vitriolic mentality—were not present with Paisley on a personal level.

---

[124] *The Revivalist* (May 1981): 11.

Paisley's fundamentalism was theological; he stuck to the theological issues and did not display that same mentality, although aspects of his life and ministry gave the opposite impression.

What was obvious to anyone who knew Paisley is that he had an amazing liberty in the gospel and he allowed others that same liberty. He enjoyed his Saviour and lived in the grace of the gospel. Many other fundamentalists, and indeed some of Paisley's followers, do not share the same liberty and therefore they could not afford it to others. The age-old trap is that the follower, trying to emulate the leader, often goes beyond the leader. It is quite possible, that if it had not been for the political activities of Paisley many of the aspects of his life that attracted so much criticism would not have surfaced.

The lives of these men, their personalities and influence, are phenomena that writers and historians have tried to unravel for a long time. The fact is these men were extremely complex personalities. Arnold Dallimore, in defense of T. T. Shields, wrote, "T. T. Shields was two personalities. Many persons who saw him in one could not possibly believe that he possessed also the other."[125] The same sentiments have been expressed of both McIntire and Paisley.

One phenomenon associated with these men, perhaps linked to their sense of divine destiny, was that they made such a deep impression in the gospel that many people who felt hurt by them could not bring themselves to speak ill of them. Many had such deep emotional ties that it became impossible for them to think objectively. They could see the faults but could not see their way clear to deal with them correctly or they graciously drew a cloak of secrecy over them.

---

125 Dallimore, "Thomas Todhunter Shields: Baptist Fundamentalist."

I speak from personal experience. My father was deeply hurt by Paisley in his early ministry. Yet, growing up in my father's home, I never heard it mentioned. I did not hear about one particular incident between my dad and Paisley until I came to North America and heard it from some of my senior colleagues who had been present at the time of the incident.[126]

I recently discovered a similar experience in the life of D. A. Carson, the New Testament scholar from Trinity Evangelical Divinity School. Carson's biography of his father speaks of his father being hurt by T. T. Shields. Similarly, Carson grew up in a home where his father and mother never spoke ill of Shields. Carson heard about the incident in history class in Bible college.[127]

Such was the effect that these men had on people, especially those who were close to them, that although those people saw many faults, they overlooked them and any hurt they might have suffered because of them.

The last seven years of Shields' life in the late 1940s and early 1950s, was a period of particular divisiveness in his ministry. One prominent fundamentalist leader, who obviously had difficulties with Shields, wrote to encourage him with these gracious words:

> So many focus their attention on the things they do not agree with, and lose sight of the underlying love and loyalty to the Person of Christ…. That which has drawn my heart to you has by far outweighed anything concerning which I have not seen eye to eye. Your

---

126 Alan Dunlop, *From Out A Poor Cradle* (Portadown: Alan Dunlop, 2010), 135–137.
127 D. A. Carson, *Memoirs of an Ordinary Pastor: The Life and Reflections of Tom Carson* (Wheaton: Crossway, 2008), 59.

exaltation of the Lord Jesus has charmed my soul, and I praise God for you and your great ministry.[128]

John Gill (1697–1771) was vigorously opposed to the ministry of George Whitefield and was accused of being a bigot in how he dealt with certain controversial subjects. His biographer, John Rippon, explains these rough edges in the personality of Gill rather quaintly:

> The doctor has been accused of bigotry, by some, who were unacquainted with his real temper and character…. If in any parts of his controversial writings, the doctor has been warmed into some little neglects of ceremony towards his assailants, it is to be ascribed, not to bigotry…but to that complexional sensibility, inseparable, perhaps, from human nature in its present state; and from which, it is certain, the apostles themselves were not exempt. [129]

Fundamentalist leaders were certainly guilty of "little neglects of ceremony"—and some not so little. We must remember that they were merely men and we should not elevate them, as some too often did, above their station. Some of the complexities of these men will never be understood. But I hope for those who are willing to hear graciously and humbly, the picture is a little clearer. In the interest of honesty we must recognize their faults; in the interest of history, and indeed of the future, we must understand their faults; and, in the interest of charity, we must "suffer long and be kind" (1 Corinthians 13:4).

---

128 See J.B. Rowell letters in the Rowell Archives presently in the author's possession.
129 John Rippon, *A Brief Memoir of the Life and Writings of the Late Rev. John Gill* (1838, reprint; Gano Books, 1992), 139–140.